Blessings beyond the Blue
And the Horror beneath the Grave

By
Pastor James L. Monteria

CLM Publications & Publishing, LLC
P.O. Box 932 Chesterfield, VA 23832

All rights reserved. No part of this book may be reproduced without written permission from the publisher except for use of brief review for furthering of the Kingdom of God unless otherwise indicated; all Scriptures are taken from the King James Version of the Bible

CLM Publications & Publishing, LLC
P.O. Box 932
Chesterfield, VA 23832
www.clmpublication.info
ISBN: 978-0-9897704-2-2

Library of Congress Catalog-in-Publication Data: 2010902849

Cover Design/Graphics: Shelly E. Middleton
Author: James L. Monteria
Associate Editor: Jennifer Powell
Special Project: Sandra Alexandra, Susan Bischoff
Published by CLM Publications & Publishing, LLC

Copyright © 2015 by CLM Publications & Publishing, LLC
Printed in the United States of America; All rights reserved under International Copyright Law. Contents and cover may not be reproduced in whole or in part in any form without the expressed written consent of the publisher.

Table of Contents
"Blessings beyond the Blue"
And the Horror beneath the Grave

Section I

Introduction   Page   1

1) Location Heaven, Heaven is a real place   Page   6
2) The Glorious Atmosphere of Heaven   Page   8
3) The Glorious Throne of God   Page 11
4) Angels and their responsibilities   Page 15
5) Culture in Heaven (People in Heaven)   Page 19
6) Special buildings for Babies in Heaven   Page 26
7) Praise and Worship in Heaven   Page 28
8) Records Rooms of Heaven   Page 32
9) Flowers, Mansions and Castles in Heaven   Page 36
10) Wardrobes in Heaven   Page 43
11) Activities of Fun Heaven   Page 45
12) Storehouses in Heaven   Page 50
13) Various Kinds of Food in Heaven   Page 55
14) Animals in Heaven   Page 58
15) Communication, Transportations
    and Invention in Heaven   Page 61
16) Heavenly Creative Inventions   Page 66

Table of Contents
"Blessings beyond the Blue"
And the Horror beneath the Grave

Section II

Horror beneath the Grave

17) Hell and its Location	Page 69
18) The Entrance to Hell and (Portals to Hell)	Page 75
19) Cells, Pits and Rooms of Hell	Page 77
20) Creatures of Hell	Page 82
21) The place called Outer Darkness	Page 87
22) Types of Torment in Hell	Page 90
23) Hell Invention and activities of Hell	Page 94
24) Bottomless Pit and Lake of Fire	Page 100
25) The Structure of Hell	Page 104
26) What is it like being in Hell?	Page 110
27) How to get to Heaven from where you live and escape Hell?	Page 133
Heavenly Decision	Page 135
Endnotes	Page 137
About the Author	Page 139

Acknowledgement

First and foremost, I would not even know God, or be able to write anything about Him, were it not for His grace and mercy! I have come to appreciate the grace of God, the Lordship of Jesus Christ, and the Holy Spirit's presence in my life and my ministry, even more than words could express.

Foreword

Many times people in the natural get excite about going on vacation to visit this place or that; they do their research in an effort to find out the best place to visit. In examining people via various questions about heaven it seems that everybody wants to go to Heaven and not hell, but very few of them know anything about heaven. My thinking is this if you want to spend eternity somewhere at least you would want to learn as must as you possible could about that place. In the next few pages I would like to share some of the exciting things that I have learn about Heaven, and the wonderful thing that Our loving God has prepared for those that love him, and have prepared themselves to spend eternity with Him.

Many Christians are excited about going to Heaven because they will receive a new heavenly body that will never grow old. There will be no more pain; no wrinkles in their faces, their teeth will be very white, and there will be no gray hair. The radiance of youth will glow from our eyes, and the average age will be thirty. We will walk on streets of gold, these are just a few basic things that God has for His family.

Psalms 16:11

Thou wilt shew me the path of life: in thy presence is fulness of joy; at thy right hand there are pleasures for evermore.

Blessings beyond the Blue

1 Corinthians 2:9; *"But as it is written, Eye hath not seen, nor ear heard, neither have entered into the heart of man, the things which God hath prepared for them that Love him."*

Introduction

Over the past ten years, Pastor Monteria has had the pleasure of researching, studying, and reading about individuals who have had the privilege of visiting heaven then returned to earth to share what they saw. Heaven is a place that has been talked about frequently; we have heard about heaven for many years and it is the place where many hope to go when their time here on earth is over. Heaven is spoken of in the Bible and by all Christians. We hear that heaven is a place where we shall live eternally.

What do we really know about heaven?

First we need to define the term "Heaven." When heaven is used in the Holy Scripture, it usually refers to one of three realms:

1. The immediate atmosphere ***First Heaven***
2. The outer space (sun, moon, and stars) ***Second Heaven***
3. The home of God ***Third Heaven***

As a result of examining the scripture, we see the Bible speaks of more than one heaven. The Scripture declares that Jesus passed through the heavens (plural) and scripture also declares Paul was taken up to the third heaven. If the Scriptures declare there is a third heaven, there must also be a first and second heaven. The Bible does not, however, mention a first and second heaven.

1. The Atmospheric Heaven - The First Heaven

The atmospheric heavens include the air we breathe as well as the space immediately surrounding the Earth. The technical term for this is the "troposphere." It extends about twenty miles above the Earth. The space above this is called the "stratosphere." The Scripture uses the term *heaven* to describe this area. In Genesis 7:23 God said… "I will destroy humanity whom I have created from the face of the earth, both humans and beasts, creeping thing and birds of heaven."

2. The Celestial Heaven - The Second Heaven

This use of the term *heaven* refers to outer space or the stellar heaven, which includes the sun, moon, and stars.

The Sun, Moon, and Stars are said to be in heaven. The Scriptures speaks of heavenly spheres beyond that which is invisible from the earth. It is called the heavens of heavens.

3. Heavens of heavens

The Home of God - The Third Heaven

The Bible is clear that God cannot be limited to any one geographical place. Yet the Scripture also teaches us there *is* a certain geographical place where God resides.

A) Stephen knew he was going into the presence of the Lord. (Acts 7:55-56)

B) Heaven is called the presence of God. (Acts 7:49)

The Bible Talks about Visions

Some of the questions that naturally come to mind when people hear of visions or going to Heaven are: "Is this for today?" and "Do people really have visions?"

How can we know if these things are from God or not? The Bible is the authority to which we can go concerning all spiritual activity. Within the Bible, we have examples of different men and women being allowed to visit Heaven. One of the first examples is Moses, who was shown various things in Heaven that he was to make after his visit.

On the day of Pentecost, 40 days after Jesus returned to Heaven following His resurrection from dead, the apostle Peter quoted a prophecy given hundreds years earlier by the prophet Joel. Peter said that this prophecy was now to be fulfilled. The Last Days referred to by Joel and Peter actually began on the Day of Pentecost, and continues to this day.

Peter proclaims:

In Acts 2: 16-18, Peter proclaims: *"But this is that which was spoken by the prophet Joel; 17 And it shall come to pass in the last days, saith God, I will pour out of my Spirit upon all flesh: and your sons and your daughters shall prophesy, and your young men shall see visions, and your old men shall dream dreams: 18 And on my servants and on my handmaidens I will pour out in those days of my Spirit; and they shall prophesy:"*

Paul proclaims:

In **2 Corinthians 12:1-2,** Paul proclaims:

> *"It is not expedient for me doubtless to glory. I will come to visions and revelations of the Lord. 2 I knew a man in Christ above fourteen years ago, (whether in the body, I cannot tell; or whether out of the body, I cannot tell: God knoweth;) such an one caught up to the third heaven.*

Visits to Heaven are Biblical:

The Prophet Isaiah wrote about one of these fortunate ones in the Book of Isaiah, chapter six, verse one through four. The Apostle Paul wrote about another in the twelfth chapter of 2 Corinthians. The Apostle John, as has been recorded in the book of Revelation, also went to Heaven. His visit was preceded by a personal visit from the Lord Jesus Christ, Who said:

> *"I am Alpha and Omega, the beginning and the ending, saith the Lord, which is, and which was, and which is to come, the Almighty."* **Revelation 1:8.**

Many times people in the natural get excite about going on vacation to visit this place or that; they do their research in an effort to find out the best place to visit. In examining people via various questions about heaven it seems that everybody wants to go to Heaven and not hell, but very few of them know anything about heaven. My thinking is this if you want to spend eternity somewhere at least you would want to learn as must as you possible could about that place. In the next few pages I would like to share some of the exciting things that I have learn about Heaven, and the wonderful thing that Our loving God has prepared for those that love him, and have prepared themselves to spend eternity with Him.

> *"Let not your heart be troubled: ye believe in God, believe also in me. ² In my Father's house are many mansions: if it were not so, I would have told you. I go to prepare a place for you. ³ And if I go and prepare a place for you, I will come again, and receive you unto myself; that where I am, there ye may be also.* **John 14:1-3;**

In studying about Heaven, the wonderful place that God has prepared for those of us who are believers. when we talk about heaven, we must understand that there are three Heavens, and we are to look forward to going to the Third Heaven. There, we will experience the fullness of His presence and His pleasures forevermore.

The Bible says: Heaven is a place of eternal pleasure. The Lord delights in pleasing His children. He wants us to be happy.

We will have heavenly bodies that will never grow old. They will be incapable of experiencing pain no wrinkles in our faces, our teeth will be white, no gray hair. The radiance of youth will glow from our eyes. Our pasture will be straight and even. We will be completely new in every respect, and it will be wonderful!

1 Corinthians 15:52-54;

> *"In a moment, in the twinkling of an eye, at the last trump: for the trumpet shall sound, and the dead shall be raised incorruptible, and we shall be changed. [53] For this corruptible must put on incorruption, and this mortal must put on immortality. [54] So when this corruptible shall have put on incorruption, and this mortal shall have put on immortality, then shall be brought to pass the saying that is written, Death is swallowed up in victory."*

> ***Heaven is prepared place for a prepared people;***
> ***Will you be there?***

Chapter 1
Location Heaven

Many books have been written by several authors that proclaim they have visited heaven and that heaven is very real. Dr. Gary Wood states, "The Bible gives us the dimensions of that city. It is 2.7 billion cubic miles in circumference. It is 2, 250,000 square miles at its base of perimeter, and is 78,000 stories high. Can you imagine the dimensions and magnitude of this *Place Called Heaven?*"[2]

Heaven has enough housing, mansions, and castles to accommodate one hundred trillion people. That is more people that have ever lived on earth at any one time. Maybe you can recall from the Bible that Jesus said, "In my Fathers' house are many mansions." [1]

Mary K. Baxter, spoke about heaven's population and how orderly it is. In one area of heaven she saw saintly men who wore white robes. She also saw people from all nations of the earth. She saw families praising God as they walked on the holy hills of heaven.

Mary K. Baxter stated that "The architecture of heaven was designed and built in eternity past by the eternal God." She goes on to say, "In one part, she saw what looked like an entire block of the city of heaven. The buildings were very large, and across the top of each was a huge impressive crown made of many jewels."[4]

Choo Thomas is one of the several authors that proclaim to have first-hand knowledge on what Heaven is like. Choo Thomas did not experience Heaven through death.

Instead, Choo Thomas states once she turned her life over to Christ, He has taken her on some remarkable journeys including Heaven. "Heaven is a prepared place for a prepared people." Coo Thomas has been given experiences from God and is prepared. Her position is to get others prepared.

"A huge wall of jasper surrounds the City of Heaven. It is beautiful. Some of the same things that were created on earth are in Heaven. Lush valleys, mountains, streams, even snow without cold, unknown fragrances, flowers, and colors; colors that seem transparent"[3]

There is no death in Heaven. Nothing breaks down or corrupts. No shadows or places of darkness, because God is light and God radiates the light beyond human reasoning.

There is more life in Heaven. All desires are met in Heaven. All desires dream, and all those never even thought of. Families are united and happy. Not like one would think or imagine happiness like on earth. [3]

> *"Let not your heart be troubled: ye believe in God, believe also in me. [2] In my Father's house are many mansions: if it were not so, I would have told you. I go to prepare a place for you. [3] And if I go and prepare a place for you, I will come again, and receive you unto myself; that where I am, there ye may be also. [4] And whither I go ye know, and the way ye know."* **John 14:1-4**

Chapter 2
The Glorious Atmosphere of Heaven

Mary K. Baxter enlightens us on the first, second and third views of heaven. "First, there is an atmospheric heaven. This is the atmosphere around the earth. It is where the birds fly and the wind blow. This is where showers, storms, mists, vapors, and clouds are formed."[4]

"The sky is the place the angel was referring to in Acts 1:11 when he asked the disciples why they were "*gazing up into heaven.*" Jesus, when he was talking to his Father, "*lifted up his eyes to heaven*" (John 17:1), or toward the sky."

"The second heaven is the heaven of space. This is the region of the sun, the moon, and the stars. It is mentioned in the Bible in many places. One of the places in the Bible which Mary K. Baxter shares is taken from Deuteronomy 4:19,

> "*And take heed, lest your lift your eyes to heaven, and when you see the sun, the moon, and the stars, all the host of heaven, you feel driven to worship them and serve them, which the Lord your God has given to all the peoples under the whole heaven as a heritage*" **Deuteronomy 4:19**

The third heaven is the heaven that remains unknown to us here on earth. It is a heaven that is passed the sky and unseen from standing on the ground and looking upward. Heaven is the region often spoken of as the immediate presence of God. Heaven is where God lives. In 1 Kings 8:30, heaven is called the dwelling place of God. In Psalms 11:4, it is called God's holy temple and the place where His throne is."[4]

Bishop Earthquake Kelly, in his book "Bound to Lose Destined to Win" with Diana Stone, said the angels in the golden vessel that carried him gently away as he was praising God that he was saved. It seemed that a mere second passed before he found himself in Paradise. The angels took him out of the vessel and He stood next to an angel dressed in gold. The angel said to him "walk around."[7]

Bishop Kelly said he could not find words in his vocabulary to adequately describe what he saw and experienced, but he tried his best to explain it. Indescribable beauty was everywhere he looked. In front of him was lush and perfectly manicured grass that was striking green color that he had every laid his eyes on.

He said that it looked as though somebody had gotten on their hands and knees to cut each blade of grass the same length. Each blade sparkled from what appear to be a purplish-green jewel embedded in each blade. He walked on the grass and found that it was softer than cotton. The blades of grass swayed to the music that seemed to be coming from a beautiful building. The trees were enormous. He saw trees that reminded him of weeping willows trees, and their branches swayed to the music as they appeared to be praising God."[7]

The music and the singing were outstanding. Nothing he had ever heard on earth can compare to music in Paradise. The sound doesn't simply go into your ears; but it permeates your entire body. The music became part of your whole being and seems to settle inside of you.

Even the flowers appeared to have a voice. The most beautiful flowers on earth look like as though they are drawn with crayons compared to the flowers in Paradise.

The colors are more intense and vibrant, and the flowers larger and livelier than anything he had ever seen on earth.

There was not one shadow in Paradise. Radiant light shone with dazzling brilliance and illuminated everything as far as he could see. With every breath he took, his entire being filled with a fragrant aroma that surpassed anything you could imagine. Everything in Paradise is a breathing masterpiece of perfection. There is nothing that can be compared. [7]

Chapter 3
The Throne of God

Psalm 11:4 *tells us that "His Throne is in Heaven"*

Isaiah 66:1 states *"that Heaven is His throne."*

Revelation 4:2 *"reveals that the throne is set in Heaven and that One sits upon it."*

Revelation 20:11 *describes it as a "great white throne."*

What is God's Throne Like?

Mary K. Baxter describes the glorious throne of God in great detail. "God's throne was *"high and lifted up"* (Isaiah 6:1). The River of Life flowed in its beauty and purity from under the base and the glory of God overshadowed the throne. It appeared that lightning, thunder, and voices were all around the throne. She goes on to say, "she saw a rainbow arching above and around God's throne *"in appearance like an emerald"* (Revelation 4:3) "The brilliant glorious hues of the rainbow were mixed with light, producing dazzlingly intense colors.

Mary K. Baxter described the varied colors of light as signals of glory and power. Furthermore, she, states, "Blazes of splendor flashed from the throne. Beams of glory radiated from it. So much of heaven seems transparent, and those illustrious beams that come forth from God's throne are filled with light that is reflected in every part of paradise!" [4]

A Door into Heaven

Revelation 4:1-6; the Message Translation.
> *"Then I looked, and, oh! – a door open into Heaven. The trumpet voice, the first voice in my vision, called out, "Ascend and enter. I'll show you what happens next.[2-6] I was caught up at once in deep worship and, oh! – a Throne set in Heaven with One Seated on the Throne, suffused in gem hues of amber and flame with a nimbus of emerald. Twenty-four thrones circled the Throne, with Twenty-four Elders seated, white-robed, gold crowned. Lightning flash and thunder crash pulsed from the Throne. Seven fire-blazing torches fronted the Throne (these are the Sevenfold Spirit of God). Before the Throne it was like a clear crystal sea.*

Jesse Duplantis shares his initial view of God's throne that he could see off in a distance. God's Throne was high and lifted up, and could be seen from every direction. He states that, "The closer he got to the Throne of God, the weaker he became, because of the glory of God." He also states that, "when people are coming to God's Throne, you see God's anointing on them, from the different levels. But when you get to the throne, nothing compares to the glory of God." The light from God's throne was overwhelming and when Jesse was able to look in the direction of the light that is when he saw Him.

He saw God, sitting on the throne. The light that came from Him was so bright that His face couldn't be seen, only his feet. The light was so intense. But Jesse looked again, and he saw the lower part of His hand, and it is huge! His body, the form of it, is sort of like energy, spirit.

There's a wall around the Throne, but the Throne is higher than the wall that's why you can see the Throne in every direction, from a distance. And that power, that energy-like smoke of God, cover all around the chair of the Throne itself.

    Jesse heard a sound, *Whoooooosh*! There was a massive amount of energy in that place. That's the only way he could explain it. It was God's power! He hear that noise, and then the energy goes back into Him. There is smoke and power and noise, the place is noisy! And angels are hollering. The angels with wings were circling the Throne, singing and shouting, "The Great God Jehovah! Every time they circled the Throne they praised God because they saw a new facet of Him they had never seen before. And they express what they see by saying "Holy! Holy! Holy!" That's how vast God is!

Even though the angels have been flying around God's Throne since the beginning of their existence, they are still seeing new revelations of His character, His love and His glory!

There was a cloud that looked like smoke going up from the Throne and Jesse heard that massive sound, *Whoosh*! It was power like he has never experienced in his life. Then he saw God's finger barely move and when it moved, an angel that was flying near Him was thrown up against a wall. *Bam*! It didn't hurt the angel, but Jesse felt if God just moved a little the universe could be annihilated.[5]

The Throne Room of God

Roberts Liardon who was eight years old when he visited heaven from his book *"We saw Heaven"* shared another unique aspect of another building. This one was very large and had a particularly strange appearance to him. He became very curious about this building because lightning flashed into it, and he heard rumblings of thunder from within. Usually, Roberts asked Jesus question in an audible voice, and Jesus would answered him audibly. This time, however, Roberts just thought, and wonder what that building is, and the answer came to him immediately. "It is the throne room of God."

Another unique aspect of this building was the seven rows of flowers in front. They lined the pathway up to the door. The colors of those flowers changed constantly into all the colors of the rainbow. Every flower, bud, and leaf was uniform in size. Also, in front of this building were 12 trees, not trees such as that grow on earth, but Heaven's trees. Roberts saw trees of wisdom that bears the fruit of wisdom, the trees of love that bears the fruit of love, and so forth.

Revelation 22:2 New Living Translation
"It flowed down the center of the main street. On each side of the river grew a tree of life, bearing twelve crops of fruit, with a fresh crop each month. The leaves were used for medicine to heal the nations."

Roberts Liardon saw two warrior angels standing in front of the door. Each held a sword, and the blades of these swords were flames of fire. The two angels always stand outside the throne room with their flaming swords fully lit. [6]

Chapter 4
Angels and their Responsibilities

Psalms 103:19-21; *"The LORD hath prepared his throne in the heavens; and his kingdom ruleth over all. Bless the LORD, ye his angels, that excel in strength, that do his commandments, hearkening unto the voice of his word. Bless ye the LORD, all ye his hosts; ye ministers of his, that do his pleasure."*

John 1:50-51; *"Jesus answered and said unto him, Because I said unto thee, I saw thee under the fig tree, believest thou? thou shalt see greater things than these. And he saith unto him, Verily, verily, I say unto you, Hereafter ye shall see heaven open, and the angels of God ascending and descending upon the Son of man."*

Hebrew 1:14; *"Are they not all ministering spirits, sent forth to minister for them who shall be heirs of salvation?"*

Sometimes paintings and other artwork give us misleading impression of angels, that they are chubby. The Bible has a lot to say about the subject of angels, and there are primarily four verses that I want to mention as we share from different individuals that have had the experience of visiting heaven.

Roberts Liardon state, "When he stood on the street of Heaven talking to people, Angels would walk up to them and their wing would move and hear a sound. Also, Roberts noticed that Angels acted differently in the presence of Jesus than people did. Where people were reverent, but talkative and friendly with Jesus, the Angels were almost silent, respectful, and reserved in His presence. He believes this is due to the fundamental difference between angels and humans."[6]

Choo Thomas affirms that angels are in heaven and here on earth. Angels are God's messengers. Angels are visiting us on earth to assure us of God's love. The angels also come to warn us that we are living in the last days. [3]

Mary K. Baxter, when angels are thought about; her vision is usually that of white robes and wings, and maybe a halo. She gives us some insight on angels and states "In heaven, the angels of God were there by the thousands. Some had wings and some didn't."

She also observed on one of her journeys to heaven that the angels were always busy performing detailed tasks. Each angel had a special assignment and certain jobs to do. But the one thing that the angels had in common is they were always praising God as they went about their business.

Mary K. Baxter also gives us an example of some of the duties of the angels. "When new souls come to heaven, angels meet them and lead them immediately through the River of Life. The angels escort the new souls to a place where other angels outfit them with gowns of salvation, which are robes of righteousness. Then the angelic guides take them to the room of crowns, where each person is fitted with a crown."[4]

Roberts Liardon states… "The Angels he saw in Heaven were tall and strong; they appeared to be from six to eight feet tall and were dressed according to their position. Some Angels have wings, but some did not. Roberts, shares his knowledge about angels and how all angels are not the same. He states, "Angels are sent from almighty God. They bring messages of healing and deliverance.

They do not speak for themselves, but are always under the authority of God. They are perfectly holy and they always obey the word of God." He enlightens us on how the Bible classifies them into a number of groups. Included in the groups are the cherubim, the seraphim, the archangel, and the common angel. Also, there are warrior angels and messenger angels.

They are classed as a different order of being. They protected the Garden of Eden with flaming swords after Adam and Eve had been put out of Eden to live on the earth.

According Genesis 3:24;

> "So he drove out the man; and he placed at the east of the garden of Eden Cherubims, and a flaming sword which turned every way, to keep the way of the tree of life."

The cherubim are described particularly in the Book of the prophet Ezekiel.

According Ezekiel 1:10, 10:14;

> *The cherubim each* "As for the likeness of their faces, they four had the face of a man, and the face of a lion, on the right side: and they four had the face of an ox on the left side; they four also had the face of an eagle."

The **Seraphim** are described in Isaiah chapter 6:2;

> "Each one had six wings; with twain he covered his face, and with twain he covered his feet, and with twain he did fly."

At the top of the angelic hierarchy are the chief angels, known as archangels.

These angels rule over entire kingdoms. The Bible names three of them: Michael, the prince of Israel; Gabriel who stands before Almighty God and he announced the birth of Jesus to His mother, Mary; and lucifer, the angel who rebelled against God and was cast down from Heaven with one third of the angels"[6]

Dr. Gary Wood states that Angels are Gods messengers who radiate the love and glory of God. Angels are to keep charge over those on earth. They obey God by sharing God's eternal message here on earth. There are Angels that are assigned to catch the tears of the saints.[2]

Every time a child of God prays earnestly and a tear drops, an Angel is there to catch those tears and deliver them to God and set them at the Throne. Same as with our praise; the Angels collect our praises and present them to God as sweet smelling incense. Angels receive the prayers from earth and bring them into the Throne room of God. [2]

Our Guardian Angels

It is true; however, that each of us is assigned an angel to be our guardian. Every one of us has at least one, and during different seasons and circumstances in our lives, more may be assigned by God to us. Matthew 18:10 reveals:

Matthew 18:10
> *"Take heed that ye despise not one of these little ones; for I say unto you, that in heaven their angels do always behold the face of my Father which is in heaven."*

The Bible states that the angels are innumerable, (See Revelation 5:11).

Chapter 5
Culture in Heaven (People in Heaven)

Revelation 5:7; *"After this I beheld, and, lo, a great multitude, which no man could number, of all nations, and kindreds, and people, and tongues, stood before the throne, and before the Lamb, clothed with white robes, and palms in their hands;*

What beings are in heaven?

God is there, Second Chronicles 6:18 say that Heaven is His dwelling place, and Deuteronomy 26:15 reveal it to be His holy habitation. Heaven *is* my throne, and earth *is* my footstool: what house will ye build me? Saith the Lord: or what *is* the place of my rest? Acts 7:49

Jesus is there because Hebrews 9:24 says He has entered into Heaven itself and appears in God's presence for us now; and the Holy Spirit is there according to John 1:32 where John the Baptist saw Him descending from Heaven like a dove."[5]

In addition to the Godhead, angels are there according to Revelation 8:10 and 8:13 and are referred to in many places such as Deuteronomy 17:3 as the host of Heaven. Revelation 5:13 refers to *"every creature which is in heaven,"* and Philippians 2:10 speaks of every knee, of things in Heaven, bowing to the name of Jesus.

And, of course, there are the believers who now dwell in Heaven, according to:

> Hebrews 12:23, who are referred to as *"the general assembly and the church of the firstborn"* and *"the spirits of just men made perfect."*

> Ephesians 3:15 calls them *"the family in Heaven."*

Psalm 89:6 makes it clear that none of the others beings in Heaven can even compare with God!" [5]

The Paradise of God;

Genesis 2:8-10;
> *"And the LORD God planted a garden eastward in Eden; and there he put the man whom he had formed. ⁹ And out of the ground made the LORD God to grow every tree that is pleasant to the sight, and good for food; the tree of life also in the midst of the garden, and the tree of knowledge of good and evil. ¹⁰ And a river went out of Eden to water the garden; and from thence it was parted, and became into four heads."*

Note - Paradise of God was not lost, but was move under the earth, this was the place that Jews who die in faith believing in the coming Messiah went. Also this was the place that Jesus spoke of when He said to the thief on the cross today you will be me Paradise. The scripture reveals that when the poor bagger who would sit at the rich man gate and the dogs would lick his sores. Died and went to Abraham Bosom, which is Paradise that was move to under the earth. When the rich man died he went to hell, and could see the poor bagger in Abraham bosom (Paradise).

When Jesus died, and through His death, burial, and resurrection paradise was relocated to Heaven, and the people who were there as recorded in Revelation 2:7 and Matthew 27:52-53.

> *"He that hath an ear, let him hear what the Spirit saith unto the churches; To him that overcometh will I give to eat of the tree of life, which is in the midst of the paradise of God."* Revelation 2:7.

Matthew 27:52-53;

> "And the graves were opened; and many bodies of the saints which slept arose, ⁵³ and came out of the graves after his resurrection, and went into the holy city, and appeared unto many."

The Bible revels that Heaven is also known as Paradise (see Luke 23:43). In it a place planned for man's eternal happiness. Man's sin, however has caused him to lose his relationship with God and his place of paradise. [6]

Will we know each other in Heaven?

In the example listed below, we share how various family members have passed, and when other family had a visit to Heaven was able to recognizes them and speak with them.

Bishop Earthquake Kelly saw his son who was killed in a carjacking.

Bishop Earthquake Kelly, in his book "Bound to Lose Destined to Win" with Diana Stone, said the angels in the golden vessel that carried him gently away as he was praising God that he was saved. It seemed that a mere second passed before he found himself in Paradise. As he continued the tour, there were a lot of great and wonderful things that he saw, but as he stood upon the crystal river bank, he look and saw another piece of land that was just as lovely from where he was standing. It was then that he saw a figure walking toward him.

Bishop Kelly was thrilled to see that it was his son, Scott! He was as handsome as ever with his big locks of hair. Bishop was elated! He cried out, "Scott, it's you! It's you! You're alive!" "Yes, Dad, I'm alive."

See back on December 7, 1998 Scott was killed when a guy carjack a car with Scott and Curtis, Jr. As Bishop Kelly visited Heaven in 2006 he saw his son Scott in Heaven. Bishop Kelly says to his "Son, this place is something! He replied, Dad, you and Mom told us for years about this place. It's so much better than anything you described." 7

Bishop Kelly asked his son, Scott "How can I cross over there? Is there a boat or something? He asked him. Scott replied "There's no boat coming for you, Dad. You can't cross this river because you must go back and finish the work God has for you to do. After Scott spoke to his dad, another man came and stood in front of him.

It was Elder Shumate, a man who died in 2002 and was a father to him in the Lord. Bishop Kelly said, is that you Elder Shumate, He replied, "Son, you can't come over this side yet. Your time is not now. You must go back. Bishop Kelly states, He saw other men and women of God whom he had known on earth." 7

Now we can understand what David meant when he said in 2 Samuel 12:16-23;

> *"My son can't come to me, but someday I'm going to him"*

Jesse Duplantis and the people he met in heaven.

One of the first persons the Jesse Duplantis met, after arriving in Heaven was Abraham, as Jesse described him, Abraham was a big barrel-chested man, He seemed of great age, yet he was young looking. There were no wrinkles in his face.

"Abraham said to Jesse after introducing himself, Paradise is my place, He meet all the people who come here, because Paradise is my bosom." 5

Jesse Duplantis, said that after he met Jesus, Jesus said, "Jesse, I want you to meet another king. He recognized him as the man that he had seen earlier. He had reddish hair and a beard. Jesse said he knew immediately it was David. As he approached them, David spoke to Jesus, "To the great king of King he bow." Jesus said, "Jesse, I want you to meet the king of Is real. The Lord said to David, "Take Jesse to his home. Show him what I have prepared for him. Then bring him to My Throne. I must go. My Father wants Me."5

David and Jesse walked into a beautiful foyer and by the corner Jesse said he saw Apostle Paul sitting with several men. On an earlier occasion Jesse had seen Jonah and he was teaching on the nature of God. 5

Jesse also saw "a family that was killed in an airplane accident," David said. "They all are here." Jesse said he was puzzled, and said he need to ask a question. Excuse me for my ignorance, but he didn't think family lived together as families. David said, "Yes, you live together," he answered, "But not as you know it on the earth. It's better than you think." 5

Rebecca Springer's vision of Heaven confirms that we will know one another in Heaven.

She confirms that those who have loved ones that have died in the Lord will know each other, and we will know them and rejoice with them in an eternity of worship and praise to the Savior of the world.

Rebecca was greeted by her uncle Frank, her dads brother who died earlier in the Lord. Frank took her hand and welcomes her to her heavenly home, He showed Rebecca through the library with rare books, and He explained that no impurity could remain in Heaven's environment. Rebecca's was visited by her parents, her mother, father, and a young sister. [8]

Loved Ones in Heaven; On her way to the river of life, Rebecca saw a young girl running towards her with her arms outstretched. It was her niece, Mae, who was radiated with joy and beauty. Mae explained that it was not only the divine life in Heaven that had transformed her; it was the frequent nearness to the Savior.

On another occasion as Rebecca began to cross the lawn between her house and her father's, she heard her name called out. Turning, she saw a tall, noble-looking man with white hair and deep blue eyes approaching her. It was Oliver, the husband of her eldest sister. [8]

Choo Thomas and the people she saw in heaven; On one occasion while visiting Heaven she saw the men who were responsible for the Bible that we have the pleasure of reading today! She had the opportunity to see the one *"Who wrote the Word of God"* They were wearing Robes and Crowns, she noticed that they were writers who were inspired to write the Bible had notebooks in their hands.

What will our bodies look like in Heaven?

Our new heavenly bodies will never grow old and will be incapable of pain. There will be no wrinkles on our faces; our teeth will be white and no gray hair. The radiance of youth will glow from our eyes. Our pasture will be straight and even. Any handicaps we experienced on earth will vanish. We will be completely new in every respect, and it will be wonderful!

How old will we be in Heaven?

In Roberts Liardon book "We saw Heaven" He states that every person that He saw looked in perfect condition and in the prime of life. They all appeared as if they were in their 30s. Perhaps this is because the Bible says we shall be like Jesus, and that was His age when He was resurrected and taken back to Heaven. So if you think that you will be too old to have fun, then that would be Heaven. Yes, there are babies and young people, but they will grow up in Heaven.

In my personal walk with the Lord I the author have had the privilege of seeing several people around the age of thirty: 1. my mother Ora Virginia Monteria, who is 81, 2. Hebert Vaughan Jr, who is 63, 3. My niece, Cassandra Wyche who is 51. In the vision they all were around thirty years old.

What a family reunion that will be!

"When we all get to heaven, what a day of rejoicing that will be, When we all see Jesus, We'll sing and shout the victory! Oh what a family reunion that will be." **I am looking forward to meeting you there!**

Chapter 6
Special buildings for Babies in Heaven

Mark 10:13-16; *"And they brought young children to him, that he should touch them: and his disciples rebuked those that brought them. [14] But when Jesus saw it, he was much displeased, and said unto them, Suffer the little children to come unto me, and forbid them not: for of such is the kingdom of God. [15] Verily I say unto you, Whosoever shall not receive the kingdom of God as a little child, he shall not enter therein. [16] And he took them up in his arms, put his hands upon them, and blessed them."*

Earlier in this century, Rebecca Spring lay very ill, near death in Canada. She had a vision of Heaven and saw her niece, Mae, there. As she and Mae walked through Heaven together, they saw little children floating and swimming upon a lake that was as smooth as glass. Later in the vision, she and a young girl she had known on earth, Mary Bates, who told Rebecca how much she wished her own heartbroken mother could see her in Heaven and be comforted. Mary's desire was that her mother would understand that her daughter was not lost to her, but would be waiting for her in Heaven when she, too joined God's saints, that is, believers in Christ.

Perhaps the most moving part of Rebecca's vision was seeing Jesus sitting beneath a flowing tree on the shore of the lake, surround by dozens of children of all ages. Some sat at His feet or leaned upon His knees and His shoulders. One tiny girl sat upon His lap, her hands was filled with flowers, as Jesus talked with them. Their faces shone with ecstasy as He told them a story and asked them questions.

Rebecca's vision confirms that Jesus has a special, tender love for the little ones of His in Heaven.[8]

In 1988, evangelist Jesse Duplantis was taken up into Heaven. While he was there, he saw a multitude of small children, singing and praising God as they played little harps. When he asked the angel who brought him there and who they were? He was told they are the children the earth did not want. As Jesse watched these children, who appeared to be from three to ten years old, he realized that they were children who had been lost to abortion. The angel explained to him that these children longed to see their mothers come to Heaven and be reunited with them. The children continued to play their beautiful music when Jesus appeared to them. His hands reached out to them as they played their harps and sang praises to Him. They hugged Him and looked up at Him in adoration. [5]

Norvel Hayes, a successful Christian businessman from Tennessee, also received a vision from the Lord that concerned children in Heaven. In his vision, which he experienced seeing a large, gray, mansion-like building? The Lord permitted him to go into many rooms there. He saw furniture designed just for little children like chairs and tables and such. It was as if the entire mansion had been prepared as a home for children. As he walked outside the building he saw beautiful flowers filled with the life of God and brilliant green grass. The presence of God in the air was so strong; every time he breathed, he experienced a divine sensation of goodness and beauty.[21]

Chapter 7
Praise and Worship in Heaven

Psalms 139:14-16; "I will praise thee; for I am fearfully and wonderfully made: marvellous are thy works; and that my soul knoweth right well. ^{15} My substance was not hid from thee, when I was made in secret, and curiously wrought in the lowest parts of the earth. ^{16} Thine eyes did see my substance, yet being unperfect; and in thy book all my members were written, which in continuance were fashioned, when as yet there was none of them."

If you are inclined to believe that we will be spending all our time in church services, in the temple of God. We need to remember that we are the church a living organism and our bodies are the temple of God. So if you believe that we will be spending all our time in church services you will be shocked. Listed below are some of the services that some of the visitors have had the privilege of attending during their visit to Heaven. (Please note that the services are about two hour long).

On one occasion during a worship service, Choo Thomas saw the Lord Jesus Christ sitting on a platform where He was dressed in pure gold. His golden crown glistened in the light and His golden robe sparkle and shone. His face was very bright, and she couldn't tell what He looked like. Then the room was filled with people who were wearing white gowns and silver crowns. They bowed in the Lord's presence, and Choo Thomas did the same as everyone else. It seems that the room began to expand in order to accommodate the rising number of people of all colors and types.

It was a moment of sacred worship and adoration before the Lord. 3

Roberts Liardon on his tour with Jesus revealed that, while they walked on, he saw a huge building resembling a convention center here on earth. Thousands of people, the saints of God, were streaming inside. The building itself had a glowing circle around it. Two angels met Jesus and Roberts escorted them down to the second row where two seats were reserved. Roberts said… "The People greeted us on the on the way to our seats, and there was not a sad face in the entire place."6

Roberts said… "You would have thought they were at a family reunion where people had not seen one another in years. They began to hug and kiss each other, saying, how are you? Glory to God! It seemed as if they were permeated with an attitude of love, they loved everyone! They didn't care what you looked like or where you were from. They just loved you, and everything they did was motivated by love. As soon as we were seated, a holy hush swept over the entire auditorium. You could literally hear a pin drop. From the right of the stage, a choir of five to six hundred "Praisers" entered, smiling as they were dressed similarly to a church choir on earth. They wore robes, and everything about their appearance was perfect. Suddenly, they began to sing and from that hushed quiet, those assembled erupted into singing and praise. "They lost all resemblance to a formal choir from that point. Their hands went up, their voices lifted in praise song, and they began to dance. Our praise services on earth could not compare."6

The congregation joined in, every person was singing with all their hearts. They were not ashamed to praise God, either. Everyone in the building lifted their hands, praised God, and leaped up and down in dance. The service seemed to last for about two hours. No individual led the worship, but everyone moved in unison. In spite of the singing and dancing, everything was done in perfect order everything. There was no "dead space" or silence. The praise never died down, but instead grew in power and momentum. When Roberts looked over at Jesus, He was smiling broadly and obviously enjoying the service. Then, all of a sudden, the praise ended abruptly, instead of diminishing gradually."[6]

Jesse shared that he had an occasion to see Jesus preach. Jesse states, "He had always thought of Jesus as being a quiet teacher, but He was full of power and preached with authority. All the people were listening. Jesus preached with great emotion." Jesse said he could see that Jesus was torn with compassion for those who were still on earth." As Jesus preached of His coming to earth, He said, "I am going to get My Body, and My Body shall reside in this place that My Father has created for us all." He began to shout: "I'm going to get your brothers! I'm going to get your sisters! I am going to get your family! I'm bringing them back to this place to live with Me forever and ever! He was a preacher full of victory, shouting and hollering! He was excited, and the people were screaming and hollering, too. As He preached to the people – even though they were in new celestial bodies fell under God's power." [5]

Jesse said… "Here on earth, we often let our time of praise die down too soon. We neglect to continue because we have not learned the sacrifice of praise and worship. To really praise God, we need to cross the "line of the spirit" where joy becomes evident in our praise. If we will do that, as believers we will see signs and wonders."[5]

Chapter 8
Records Rooms of Heaven

*Revelation 13:5, 8; "He who overcomes shall be clothed in white garments, and I will not blot out his name from the **Book of Life**; but I will confess his name before My Father and before His angels" "All who dwell on the earth will worship him, whose names have not been written in the **Book of Life** of the Lamb slain from the foundation of the world."*

*Revelation 17:8; "The beast that you saw was, and is not, and will ascend out of the bottomless pit and go to perdition. And those who dwell on the earth will marvel, whose names are not written in the **Book of Life** from the foundation of the world, when they see the beast that was, and is not, and yet is."*

Roberts Liadron shares about the books and songs in Heaven that are intended for our knowledge and enjoyment in praising God on earth, while others are designed to give not just academic knowledge, but an understanding of the times and seasons of God's plan on earth so men may cooperate with His present-day workings. These books and songs are intended to motivate mankind and bring an impartation of God's very life to those on earth.

"There is, however, a price to be paid to bring these books and songs from Heaven to earth for the benefit of the body of Christ. It is the price of walking in the Spirit being led by God' Spirit rather than submitting to those desires of ours that oppose Him."[6]

You pay this price by spending much time in prayer and loving God's Word more than earthly pleasures, knowledge, and entertainment.

The men and women who would bring these books and songs from Heaven must be able to resist both the flattering popularity that might come and the rejection by those who won't understand.

Mary K. Baxter shares her vision of the room of records and stated; "She was amazed to see a room of records in which meticulous records were being kept. The angel said that God has His angels keep records of every church service on earth and every service in a home where He is lifted up and praised."[4]

"God also keeps records on those who are out of His will. Mary K. Baxter shares that God showed her how God's angels keep records of the money that is given in church services, along with a record of the attitudes with which people contribute. He told her of people who have money but won't give to the work of the Lord." [4]

The Room of records in heaven is not just one room; there are many rooms of records. In every record room, there is an angel in charge. Everything that goes in or out of a record room must be cleared by that angel. All is done in order to the glory of God.

In one room there were ladders positioned along the walls. Shelves covered the walls and books covered the shelves. Some of the books were different shades of color. The room had the appearance of a library here on earth. There was also a beautiful desk in this particular room of records. The desk was eight feet across and four feet wide with a square cutout in the center which was overlaid with solid gold. [4]

Dr. Gary Wood also shares his experience in the room of records and states, "John took me into a very large building that looked like a library.

The walls were solid gold and sparkled with a dazzling display of light that loomed up high to a crystal, domed ceiling. He saw hundreds and hundreds of volumes of books.

Each book had a cover of beautifully carved gold with a single letter of the alphabet engraved on the outside. Many angels were reading the contents of these books. John explained to me that these books contain a record of every person's life that has ever been born, throughout history. [2]

Everything we do here on earth is recorded in these books good or bad everything. Dr. Gary Wood watched as an angel opened one of the books, and with a cloth, wiped the pages. As he did this, the page turned red and the writing vanished from the pages, leaving only a name. Dr. Gary Wood asked what that meant and was told red represents the cleansing from by the blood of Jesus, your Savior.

Revelation 3:5; *"He that overcometh, the same shall be clothed in white raiment; and I will not blot out his name out of the book of life, but I will confess his name before my Father, and before his angels."*[1]

Revelation 20:12-15; *"And I saw the dead, small and great, stand before God; and the books were opened: and another book was opened, which is the book of life: and the dead were judged out of those things which were written in the books, according to their works. [13] And the sea gave up the dead which were in it; and death and hell delivered up the dead which were in them: and they were judged every man according to their works. [14] And death and hell were cast into the lake of fire. This is the second death. [15] And whosoever was not found written in the book of life was cast into the lake of fire."* [1]

Names were transferred from these books to the *Lamb's Book of Life* and sins were erased and remembered against name of that person no more. The *Lamb's Book of Life* is for those who have received everlasting life by asking Jesus to save them. Other books were shown to Dr. Gary Wood that contained prayer requests, spiritual growth in the Lord, and a record of the number of souls that they had led to Christ. The books were all very detailed, as everything is done and made known to God.

Chapter 9
Flowers, Mansions and Castles in Heaven

> John 14:1-3; *"Let not your heart be troubled: ye believe in God, believe also in me. ² In my Father's house are many mansions: if it were not so, I would have told you. I go to prepare a place for you. 3 And if I go and prepare a place for you, I will come again, and receive you unto myself; that where I am, there ye may be also."*

Choo Thomas, shares that Jesus took her to a garden that was so vast that she could not see where it ended, and as they hiked out of the garden, along a narrow, winding road that led to a mountain vista overlooking a lush green valley. Jesus and Choo Thomas turned to go in another direction; Choo Thomas notices a beautiful river. Along the river was a rock wall, with magnificent dwellings were situated on the left side of the river. Many of those homes looked like castles where only the very wealthy might live. Jesus said to Choo Thomas, "These are houses for my special children."[2]

The Lord took Choo Thomas to a *beautiful castle*, "they got closer to the dwelling, Choo Thomas could see the streets were paved with lustrous gold and that every castle was lavishly decorated with the finest gems. It is true that the streets of heaven are paved with solid gold!" As Jesus and Choo Thomas approached one of the *castles*, the Lord opened the door for Choo Thomas to enter, the walls were constructed of multicolored precious gems that glistened and glowed in a magical way. The Lord rested on a chair as Choo Thomas went up the winding staircase that was more massive and grand than the one shown in *Gone with the Wind's* Tara plantation.

Choo Thomas was filled with a sense of wonder as she imagined the magnificence of the rooms upstairs. At the top of the staircase, she noticed that the carpeting was a plush white. As Choo Thomas enter a huge powder room that had very large sparkling mirrors everywhere. They reflected the brightness of the room and the multitude of colors that arrayed themselves spectacularly on every wall. It was a more wonderful place than any fantasy castle could be. [3]

On another occasion Jesus took Choo Thomas to a dwelling. It was a **_white mansion_** sumptuously landscaped with a profusion of colorful flowers and leafy trees. The most wonderful flowers that she had never seen grace the doorway. The doors were lovely as well, decorated with extraordinary stained glass panels. Inside the palace, everything was colorful and shiny. The great room was filled with people who were wearing beautiful gowns, and each person was wearing a crown that was set with jewels of variety.[3]

On another occasion Jesus and Choo Thomas walked pass many **_mansions and castles_**, each more exquisite than the last. As Jesus and Choo walking they stood in front of one of these dwelling, the Lord stopped emphatically. Choo Thomas knew that the Lord was going to take her inside, and she was excited beyond all measure, her heart was skipping beats as she walked up to the front steps. As her eyes were dawn to the doorknob, which was made of pure gold. Then she saw a gold plate on the front door. It had her name inscribed on it, and as she realized that it was her name she almost fainted because of this surprise, written in fancy lettering was the name "Choo Thomas."[3]

As the Lord opened the door she cried tears of gratitude and joy as her heart was overflowed with love and adoration for the Lord. As she stepped across the threshold of her mansion she was awestruck by the sparkling stone walls that lined the corridor of her mansion. She loved the red-cream-colored carpet with its round patterns, with red velvet chairs, that were so classic and sophisticated. She had red draperies that were the finest that she had ever seen.

As the Lord took His seat in one of the velvet chairs, Choo walked up the majestic stairway, savoring every single moment in her mansion. The bedroom was carpeted in pure white, and the headboard of the bed was silver with blue stone embedded decoratively along its border. The mirror on the dresser also had blue stones highlighting its brightness. The bathroom had a silver bathtub that was decorated with precious jewels of every color.

On another occasion Jesus took Choo Thomas for a walk along another road that was narrow, and as they reached the end of this narrow road way Jesus showed Choo Thomas a white fence surrounding many white buildings. They glistened with the purest white, a whiteness more brilliant than freshly fallen snow. Than Jesus took Choo Thomas by the hand and they began to fly, and landed in the fertile valley, Jesus showed Choo Thomas the pure white street were and there are beautiful <u>white houses</u> were on both sided of the street. The street was white and shiny like glass. Everything seemed so white there. The fence seemed to be much higher than the houses that Choo Thomas saw from the top of the hill narrow road way.

Choo Thomas said the Lord told her that He must show her this house, and they approached one of these houses. It had double doors with golden trim. The door was outlined with colored glass. Choo Thomas took particular notice of the knob made of pure gold! As she entered the house, she noticed that all the windows were made of stained glass. The carpeting was colorful a mixture of subdued hues and it gave the interior of the house a very classic look. The jewels that adorned the walls sparkled and shone. She felt as if she were stepping into a picture rather than a house.

Choo Thomas said that she walked up the golden stairway that had an intricate design etched into its surface. At the top of the stairs, she walked into a bedroom where a bed stood that was grander and large than any king-size bed on earth. [3] Choo Thomas stated that she walked around it and in the powder room. It was laden with gold and precious gems on every wall except one. That wall had a full-length mirror to reflect the amazing beauty of the environment. She noticed that all the rooms in this house were immense, including the powder room. In fact, everything the Lord showed her had huge rooms that were beautiful beyond all expectations.

Choo Thomas said that Jesus asked her, *"Do you like this place?"* Yes, my Lord. It's beautiful. Who will live in these houses You are showing me? Jesus said "All of my children will live in these houses I've prepared for them. They will be living here sooner than they think.

<u>The Special Pond</u>, on another occasion Jesus took Choo Thomas to visit another building that looked like the picture of medieval ***European castle.***

There was a rock wall on both side of the castle, and magnificent flowers were planted all around. Jesus and Choo Thomas entered the castle, and it had a beautiful colorfully carpeted foyer. The elegant furniture was selected to fit the color and the style of the carpeting. The walls were sparkling and shiny – so brilliantly that Choo Thomas was almost blinded. At the end of the hallway, just ahead, Choo Thomas noticed a sliding door, and she wondered what would be discovered on the other side. The Sliding glass door, did not lead into another room; rather it was a doorway to the castle garden. In the center of this glorious place was a pond.

The entire "backyard" was surrounded throughout by a rock wall, flowers of every type and description formed a sea of beauty everywhere, and Choo Thomas looked she noticed a variety of fruit trees grew close to the rock wall. These trees were filled the biggest, most luscious looking fruits that she had ever seen. They were ringed by a magnificent profusion of lovely flowers scattered throughout this amazing garden were huge gray boulders that seemed to be strategically placed for sitting and resting.[3]

Jesse Duplantis stated that in his visit to heaven he saw his *mansion*. He states, "When he and David walked up, he looked at the grounds. There was a water fountain in the front yard and manicured grass. It was the prettiest place he had ever laid his eyes on. To Jessie, the foyer of a home set the mood of a house. When he went through the front door, there were tall ceilings and crown moldings. Everything was decorated and the furniture was just the kind he liked. This place is beautiful! Jesse said they have furniture like this on the earth.[5]

David said "Yes, the Lord knew you would like it, so they put it in your home. He told you that He would give you the desires of your heart," David said. "All desires are met here. Everything has been thought of, all of your desires and some that you could not even think of." Everything was so perfect down to the last detail. It was all so beautiful! Jesse looked at more physical things in his home than anywhere else. There was marble, and there was a table in the foyer with golden eagles on it. "David," Jesse said, "There are lots of things here that look like things on the earth." "Well the earth is the Lord's taste," he answered. "Remember, He created it. So a lot of what you see there you will see here"[5].

On April 1st, as Jesus and Choo Thomas walked again on the long road and when reaching an intersection, they took a side road that meandered very close to the golden bridge that led to a beach. As they traveled this road, Choo Thomas noticed many houses situated around the water. In the back of the houses there are fruit trees of all sorts. It was a very orderly orchard. The first rows consisted of pale green trees that were filled with purple fruits. The next grouping was of larger trees with red leaves. The colors were multitudinous and blended together in a most delightful way. The array of colors was so spectacular that it took Choo Thomas breath away. There were not any mountains in this particular region of heaven only water, sand, houses and trees.

It was such a vast area that Choo Thomas couldn't see where it ended. The Lord took Choo Thomas into one of the houses. This one was greatly different from the mansions and castles that she had visited before. Its interior was quite simple, and its colors were somewhat subdued.[3]

The Lord explained "***These are beach houses for my children***" It was amazing! We'll all have vacation homes in heaven! Truly, the Lord does want His children to be happy and to enjoy His pleasures forevermore.

> Psalms 16:11 *"Thou wilt shew me the path of life: in thy presence is fullness of joy; at thy right hand there are pleasures for evermore."*

Chapter 10
Wardrobes of Heaven

Revelation 19:14 Also describes the clothing in Heaven. The riders were *"dressed in fine linen, white and clean"*

Revelation 7:9 describes 144,000 saying, *"They were wearing white robes and were holding palm branches in their hands"*

Isaiah 61:10; *"I will greatly rejoice in the LORD, my soul shall be joyful in my God; for he hath clothed me with the garments of salvation, he hath covered me with the robe of righteousness, as a bridegroom decketh himself with ornaments, and as a bride adorneth herself with her jewels."*

Revelation 13:5; *"He who overcomes shall be clothed in white garments, and I will not blot out his name from the Book of Life; but I will confess his name before My Father and before His angels."*

Is there clothing in Heaven?

The clothing that is worn in heaven is revealed through the scriptures. If you are really want to see that the serious of the wardrobes of the citizen of the Kingdom of Heaven please see Exodus chapters 21-25.

Roberts Liadron stated that "The people in Heaven wore white robes, which was the most important item of their dress; it represents the right standing with God that Jesus paid for with His blood. These robes seemed to radiate from within. Some wore different colored sashes, and still other was adorned with jewelry."[6]

In the DVD's series by Jesse Duplantis entitle "Heaven close encounter of the God kind" he states that what you wear in heaven reveal what you have accomplish for the Lord.

As Jesus visited Choo Thomas, she records in her book "Heaven is so Real" the clothing of Jesus our Lord and Savior, the King of Kings and Lord of Lords in His very first visit on January 1996 "He was wearing a <u>pure white robe</u>."[3]

On February 24, 1996, Jesus took Choo Thomas to heaven and she was directed by an angel to a little room on the side, and was surprised to discover a powder room there. A full length mirror covered the entire wall on the left side of the room, and beautiful velvet chairs were neatly arranged in front of the mirror.

A beautiful being which she perceived to be an angel stood in front of her, and opened a large walk-in closet that contained <u>many robes, gowns and crowns</u>. Each robe had <u>rich embroidered colors</u>. She thought the garments were the most <u>stunning and expensive clothing I'd ever seen</u>." [3]

Chapter 11
Fun Activities in Heaven

Psalm 16:11; *"You will show me the path of life; In Your presence is fullness of joy; At Your right hand are pleasures forevermore."*

In sharing this section with you about "Fun Activities in Heaven" Perhaps it would be nice to know how old every person will be. Again in Roberts Liardon book "We saw Heaven" He states that every person that He saw looked in perfect condition and in the prime of life. They all appeared as if they were in their 30s this is because the Bible says we shall be like Jesus, and that was His age when He was resurrected and taken back to Heaven. So if you think that you will be too old to have fun, then that wouldn't be Heaven. Yes there are babies and young people, but they get to grow up in Heaven.

On March 5, 1996 Jesus and Choo Thomas walked across a golden bridge, through a verdant valley. They follow a beautiful road that was bordered by a golden fence with many gates. Choo Thomas is now familiar with fruit trees and picturesque yellows followers, and beautiful rocks that were strewn across the fields and the fast-flowing, clear-as-crystal river that was nearby.

On March 15, 1996 Jesus and Choo Thomas descended from mountain and walked on the sand between the rocks. It was the whitest, cleanest sand that she had ever seen, and the beach was absolutely the most beautiful that she had ever seen. Some of the rocks nearby were so huge that she could not see their tops. As they walked around one of them, Choo Thomas noticed a large group of people wearing white robes. [3]

Each person was distinctly different from the other in appearance, and many children could be seen playing in the sand. Some children were holding the hands of grownups, and everyone was walking around in a playful, happy manner. Choo Thomas said it was wonderful to see a place of such brightness and joy. Jesus sat next to Choo Thomas on one of those big rocks for quite a while, simply enjoying the vibrant beauty all around them. Jesus turned to Choo Thomas and said, "I have made so many things that are similar to the things on earth so that my children can enjoy them when they come to My Kingdom, but there are many things that are not the same as things on earth. I have so many exciting surprises for My children."[3]

On April 3, "As the Lord and Choo Thomas continued to walk along the road and reached a narrow road on the left onto which they turned and proceeded. Around a little curve in the road Choo Thomas noticed a massive ocean that was so vast that it appeared to have no end. As they neared the waterfront, she noticed a high rock wall that had steps leading down to the shoreline. They went up to the wall and walked down the steps."[3]

An Endless Ocean

The edge of the sea was filled with boats, large and small. It was a marina in heaven, and each boat was chained to a thick bar. All of their hulls were white. As they got closer, she noticed every boat had a beautifully furnished cabin and windows of stained glass that resembled little churches on the water.

The Lord led her to one of the boats, and they climbed in. The interior of the cabin was immaculate, but the boat was only large enough for two people. There were two seats in the front and two steering wheels.

Choo Thomas began to remember the Lord had related to the sea, nature, and fishing during his earthly ministry. Peter, James, and John; three of his disciples, had been fishermen. He frequently preached on the shore of the Sea of Galilee and he often used fish as object lessons.

Jesus loves the sea! He loves the world of nature He created, and he wants us to enjoy it as well. In fact, when the creation took place, human beings were to live in paradise more wonderful than one could possibly imagine the Garden of Eden a place of purity, innocence, perpetual springtime, fruitfulness, peace, and joy. But because Adam and Eve sinned, they were banned from that earthly paradise. God, in his great love, however, made a way for us to regain paradise in heaven. He sent His Son Jesus to die for us. Paradise lost was regained through the death, burial and resurrection of His Son Jesus.

As a Christian we shouldn't be surprise that our heavenly home will be like the most fantastic places of earth, the oceans, forests, fields, trees, flowers, birds, animals, fruits, and rivers are there for us to enjoy just as God had created them for us in the Garden of Eden. Because of sin, the way was lost for us to enjoy such an earthly paradise, but through faith in Jesus Christ paradise will one day be restored to each of us!

Yes, Jesus loved the sea, and He loved all of nature that He created. That's why we shouldn't be surprise that heaven is the prototype of everything that is beautiful on earth. Our Lord and Master want us to enjoy the Kingdom.

It was clear that Jesus wanted Choo Thomas to enjoy the experience of a heavenly boat ride. He pushed a button and the small craft began to move, slowly at first, and then they picked up speed. She loved the breeze against her face and the cooling mist that seemed so clean and refreshing. Choo Thomas began to laugh as they sped over the sea's calm surface, and then she began to sing. She was so joyful. It was far different from any boat ride she had ever taken on earth, during which she usually had gotten seasick or very nauseated. Not this time. She was enjoying every moment of their thrilling ride.

Somehow, even though at times she was doubled over with laughter, she managed to steer them back to the docking area. They got out the boat and the Lord tied the boat back to the bar. He then said, "*Choo Thomas, you see the kingdom has many of the things you know on earth. When all my children come to my kingdom, I want them to enjoy the things I've prepared for them,*" She smiled, because she understood a little bit of what He meant."[3]

The River of Life

Roberts Liadron shares about the River of Life. He assume there is only one river in Heaven, although there may be more; He only saw one. The river of life is described in Revelation 22:1 as being crystal bright, flowing from the throne of God and the Lamb.

In Revelation 22:17, Jesus says… "He gives the pure water freely to the thirsty. It purifies you and cleanses you of the contamination of the earth life and gives you strength from its source, that place where God sits and rules as King of the universe."[6]

When Jesus and Roberts walked up to the river of life, they didn't just look at it, but walked into it. It was knee deep and perfectly clear. Unlike a river on earth, it doesn't just flow around you. It flows through you, and you feel a surge of energy come up out of that water and into your being. Then Jesus did something that is quite personal and extremely precious to Roberts, and He love to tell this part of story of tour of Heaven. The Lord Jesus, the Holy Son of God, reached over and dunked Roberts under the water of the river of Life. So he got back up, splashed Him (Jesus) and they proceeded right there to have a water fight, splashing each other and laughing. Jesus, the King of Glory, the Lamb of God took time out for little 8 year old Roberts Liardon to play with him in the river of life. Jesus and Roberts played in the river of life for a while, they got out. It was as if a giant hair dryer then began to blow and dried their clothes instantly. They put on their shoes and departed, and they began to walk past more buildings, seeing other people. [6]

Jesse Duplantis share on occasion when David the king was taken him to see his mansion, they saw this family and they were going into their mansion and then on a picnic and they invited him to join them, but because of his schedule Jesse was not permitted to go. David shared, "Yes, you live together, if they wanted to, but not as you know on the earth. It's better than you think."[5]

Chapter 12
Storehouses of Heaven

Jeremiah 33:3 *"Call unto me, and I will answer thee, and shew thee great and mighty things, which thou knowest not.*

One of the saddest days of a Christian life is when they get to heaven. The reason for this is because when they get to heaven they will see all the unclaimed blessings that should have been enjoyed while on earth. See there are many blessings our loving Heavenly Father has provided for us to enjoy in the here and now, but because of ignorance and lack of Faith a decision was made to put off the blessing until when they get to Heaven.

Roberts Liardon had the privilege of visiting Heaven at the tender age of 8 years old on a tour with Jesus. Roberts stated that he saw three storage houses, five to six hundred yards from the throne room of God. They were very long and wide and seemed to be shaped similar to one of the large chicken house you see out in countryside where hundreds of chicken are raised using his 8 years old Oklahoma vocabulary. The first storage house they walked into as Jesus shut the door behind them, Roberts says he was shock as he looked at the interior. On one side of the building he saw exterior parts of the human body, all different colors, corresponding to different ethnic groups. On the other side of the building, Roberts saw different eyes that included green, brown, blue ones-eyes and other colors. The next building contained all the parts of the human body that people on earth need, but Christians have not realized these blessings are waiting for them in Heaven.

Dr. Gary L. Wood's book "A place called Heaven" shared of walking into a long building, much like a storage building. He stated…"he was caught off guard by what he saw hanging from the walls. There were rows of legs, rows of arms, cubicles with hair and eyeballs of various colors and every part of one's anatomy was in this room. As he walked into a room that was like a nursery, and saw what looked like big globs of flesh, heaped into mounds.[2]

In the book by Jesse Duplantis book "Heaven Close Encounters of the God kind," states all of a sudden, he heard kids singing and praising God. Then he saw them carrying little harps. He asked the angels where did all these children come from? These are children that they did not want, he said. God brought them here. Jesse said, but he thought people went to heaven because they chose to go. The angel said to Jesse, "No, Jesse, children must be taught the oracles of God." Jesse says… "He saw that many people were teaching these kids, so he realized that God was using people as well as angels to teach others in heaven about Him. [5]

Then Jesse asked the angel, "Are you talking about abortions?" The angel said, "Yes". The children can't wait to see their mothers." Jesse said, "The ages of the children he saw seemed to be from about three to ten years old, and babies were off in another place. [5]

Bishop Earthquake Kelley with Diana Stone, in his book *"Bound To Lose and Destined To Win"* states… "He saw group of children of all different ages who were running, jumping, and playing.[7]

Then he saw another group of children that caught his eye. As he stood watching these children, Bishop Kelly said He heard a voice say, "You're wondering who those children are." It was clear that this voice was responding to his thoughts. Bishop Kelly was surprised that someone could read his thoughts. He looked around and, although he didn't see anybody, he knew that he was hearing the voice of the Lord. He replied, "Yes, Lord, Bishop Kelly said he was wondering who they are." "These are children who died from diseases, wars, accidents, murders, and other things that happen to children." Bishop said. "Some were stillbirths and others died from miscarriages. These are all the children that the Lord brought home to be with Him. No harm can ever come to them again."

Then the voice of the Lord choked back tears as He pointed out another group of children and said, "See those children? He had a plan for their lives. He had things for them to do. But because of selfishness of sin and the hardness of peoples' hearts, these children were aborted and sent back to me. The Lord pointed out another group of children and, with the same trembling voice said, "He sent these children to the homes of so-called Christians. He sent these children for ministry. He sent them for exhortation. He sent them to help the world. But their parents listened to the ways of the world. They listened to the wrong counsel. They thought they had financial problems and could not afford these children. They had secret abortions, thinking that nobody would find out. But nothing is hidden from me. Jesus said He see everything."[7]

Shawn Bolz' book, "The Keys to Heaven's Economy." Had an Angelic Visitation from Minister of Finance shares how in 1997, he was transported to a heavenly realm and taken to a huge warehouse. He states that he could not distinguish the ceiling or walls even though the room was enclosed. The angel who oversaw the storehouse was assigned to show him around. As he took him on a tour through different sections of the building, he was gripped by anticipation. "What is this place?" Shawn asked. His eyes lit up. The Angel smiled and replied, "This is the storehouse of Heaven."

The Department of Creative Miracles

The angel and Shawn walked down aisles of glory. It was unlike any place Shawn had ever seen, his mind almost hurt just trying to take in all the awesome landscapes. Eventually, they reached a room within the larger warehouse that reminded Shawn of a trade show that he had been to once. The aisles in this room were so large that Shawn couldn't describe all that he saw. One section was dedicated to the physical body. Aisle upon aisle displayed body parts of every type. When Shawn walked down an aisle and found a leg. It was one of tens of thousands of legs hanging a rack that almost reminded Shawn of something you'd find in a meat factory, in some odd way.

The Leg, Shawn noticed had a toe tag. But then Shawn realized all the legs on the aisle had tags. The specific tag he read bore a woman's name and had the date it would be delivered. This woman on earth would literally be restored to walking one day!

Can you image that God has already made provision for various limbs and all is need is the faith to manifest it? Shawn looked at his angelic companion and asked, "What is this room?" Shawn stated that he felt like weeping.

In the next room was the Department of Creative Miracles," he responded. He didn't need to explain it further. Surrounding me were eyeballs, ears, teeth, hair, toes, fingers, bones, muscles, organs, and so many body parts! These body parts constituted only one section of the Creative Miracles Department. There were many other kinds of creative miracles as well.[9]

Chapter 13
Various Kinds of Food in Heaven

Revelation 22:2; *"In the middle of its street, and on either side of the river, was the tree of life, which bore twelve fruits, each tree yielding its fruit every month. The leaves of the tree were for the healing of the nations.*

Some people might have problems about eating in Heaven, the Bible; however, mention the marriage supper of the lamb in Revelation 19:9; and Revelation 22:2, John writes of the tree of life that is in Heaven, bearing 12 kinds of fruits. In addition, John 21:9-14 tells us that Jesus ate fish and bread with the disciples after He was resurrected and had a transfigured body – the kind we will have in Heaven.

One of the revelations Choo Thomas shares with her readers is about the food in heaven. We eat all kinds of food here on earth. Some of us consume food that is not very healthy. We eat foods with a lot of sodium, sugar, fats and cholesterol. So, let's get clarification on what foods are eaten in Heaven. According to Choo Thomas, as Jesus and Choo Thomas walked she saw a body of water that looked like a very long, narrow river and on both sides of the river are magnificent fruit trees. On one side of the river, purple fruit was on the tree and on the other side of the river, red fruit was on the tree. She described the fruit as attractive looking and that the red fruit was in the shape of large teardrops.

On another occasion as Jesus and Choo Thomas walked across a picturesque bridge built from red wood. As they walked over it Choo Thomas stated that she looked down and saw that the stream was filled with many kinds of fish.

She asked Jesus "What are all the fish for?" Jesus replied *"This is food for the Kingdom."*[3]

On another occasion Jesus and Choo Thomas walked across a golden bridge, and walked along a hillside by a beautiful valley. A golden fence formed a boundary around the entire area, and the fence had several gates that were placed close to one another all around. This road led to a hill that was much smaller than the mountain that Jesus and Choo Thomas usually climbed. From the rising crest Choo Thomas noticed a silver river shinning in Heaven. Mountain range was filled the panorama with a beauty that only heaven could produce. The mountain seemed to be forested with evergreen trees. As Jesus and Choo Thomas descended the hillside and walked to the river of water. Choo Thomas states, "she looked down and saw all kinds of fish swimming in the river over the rocky bottom. She asked, "What are all the fish for?" The Lord replied to her saying, *"This is food for the Kingdom."*[3]

Jesse Duplantis share in his book *"Heaven Close Encounters of the God Kind"* That He saw other people step out of a chariot like the one that he was brought to Heaven in, who didn't have robes; they were wearing gowns. They started walking toward the city, but seemed to get weak. Jesse saw them walk over to the trees, pick what looked like fruit and ate it. Then they took leaves off those trees, put the leaves up to their faces and breathed in, smelling them.

Jesse asked the angel, "What's happening?" The angel said, "Some of them have not lived the life they should. They believe in God and Love Jesus, but they didn't live to their fullest potential. Jesse asked the angel, "Will they still be able to go before God's Throne?" The angel said, "Yes, God is merciful to them," he said. "But they have to be prepared to stand in the presence of the Almighty."

Jesse said then he realize that those leaves were for the healing of the nations that the Apostle John spoke of in

> Revelation 22:1,2; *"And he shewed me a pure river of water of life, clear as crystal, proceeding out of the throne of God and of the Lamb. ² In the midst of the street of it, and on either side of the river, was there the tree of life, which bare twelve manner of fruits, and yielded her fruit every month: and the leaves of the tree were for the healing of the nations."*

Jesse said, "He could see that the fruit helped those people to stay in God's Glory.

Even when Jesse began to feel weak, the angel walked over to one of those trees, picked some of its fruit and brought it back to him. Jesse said he doesn't know what kind of fruit it was, but it wasn't an apple. It was juicy and copper-colored fruit. The angel said to Jesse; "eat this fruit so you can be able to withstand the glory of God." So Jesse ate it, and he was strengthened.

Chapter 14
Animals in Heaven

> Revelation 4:7 *"And the first beast was like a <u>lion</u>, and the second beast like a <u>calf</u>, and the third beast had a face as a <u>man</u>, and the fourth beast was like a flying <u>eagle</u>."*

Are there Animals in Heaven?

Many times when teaching on the subject of Heaven there are people with the question are there animals in heaven? In examining the scriptures we see in revelation 4:7 the God himself has four living creature around his throne, *"And the first beast was like a <u>lion</u>, and the second beast like a <u>calf</u>, and the third beast had a face as a <u>man</u>, and the fourth beast was like a flying <u>eagle</u>."* Revelation 4:7, and when God told Noah about the judgment of the flood that was coming upon the earth, did He not say to gather the animals two by two. "

Yes, 2 Kings 2:11 tells of the fiery horses drawing the chariot that took the prophet Elijah up in Heaven.

> 2 Kings 2:11 *"And it came to pass, as they still went on, and talked, that, behold, there appeared a chariot of fire, and horses of fire, and parted them both asunder; and Elijah went up by a whirlwind into heaven."*

> Revelation 6:1-7; mentions, *Tells of the four horsemen, seated variously upon a white, a red, a black, and a pale horse.*

In 1998 Roberts Liardon, at the tender age of 8 years old on a tour of Heaven, Jesus and Roberts continue walking, and as they cross some hills. They saw all kinds of animals, every kind you can think of, from A to Z. The Bible talks about horses in Heaven and why would God have only one kind of animal? [6]

The most well-known reference, of course, is regarding Jesus returning to earth on a white horse, found in Revelation 19:11. When the prophet Elijah was taken up into Heaven, a fiery horse and chariot were sent down after him.

Roberts Liardon states while in Heaven, He saw a dog, a baby goat, and a lion of great strength. There were birds singing in the trees, all sizes of birds, and they seemed to be singing the same song. He could understand what they were singing. There was no communication gap. When they stopped singing, it seems as if they began to talk among themselves. There were other animals that he could see in a distance, but could not identify them. These animals neither ran from people nor tried to attack them. All were calm and peaceful, because fear cannot be found in Heaven. God's presence is so strong that there is no confusion, doubt, sickness, or worry there. [6]

Heaven is a wonderful place of peace of joy where all the animals coexist in delightful harmony.

A spectacular deer

On one occasion Jesus and Choo Thomas hiked out of the garden, along a narrow, winding road that led to a mountain vista overlooking a lush green valley. She could see animals of all sorts galloping and playing among the trees. She particularly noticed a spectacular deer that looked so strong and healthy. Choo Thomas was happy to let them know that heaven is a peaceful and glorious radiance where people and animals alike will never experience pain, hardship, death or suffering again[3]

On April 3, Jesus and Choo Thomas walked over the golden bridge and walked on the right side of a road. It was a very wide road that had a canopy of leaves overhead from the mighty trees that grew on either side of the road. This was a different road from any one they had walked on before. They walked for a long while and then a road to the right. They walked for quite a while on this road as well. [3]

Heavenly Doves

It encircled the base of a large, rocky mountain. To their left, there was a wide valley filled with green trees. The middle of the valley seemed to be filled white gravel. As Choo Thomas looked over the serene valley, she notices movement in the region of the white gravel. The area was filled with birds. She said "Lord, what kind of birds are they? Jesus said… "They are doves" Why are there so many doves here?" Jesus said…"They are very important to Me.? It was a magnificent place so large and so beautiful. As they climbed atop a solid rock wall upon which they could stand and watch the doves of heaven. They remained there for a long time, and Choo Thomas was profoundly moved by what she saw.[3]

Jesse Duplantis shared from his book "Heaven Close Encounters of the God Kind" That He saw horses, dogs, and large cats like lions. [5]

Chapter 15
Communication, Transportation and Inventions

Over the years of being a Christian, I've purpose to obey the Word of God. In continue to study on the subject of Heaven it has been so rewarding to know that one of the most importance things that God require of His children is obedience, and that God loves us beyond our wildest imaginations, desire and plans nothing but the best for His Children.

In Heaven we have two ways of communicating. Yes we will be able to continue to talk as we do here on earth using our vocabulary speaking audibly, but there is also for believe that our vocabulary will be greater than ever before. The next way of communicating that is discovered from reading after people that have visited Heaven is that when they have questions, they will obtain an answer before they ask them.

> Matthew 6:8; *"Be not ye therefore like unto them: for your Father knoweth what things ye have need of, before ye ask him."*

While here on earth we communicate via our vocabulary speaking audibly, and as a Christians we have the Holy Spirit speaking to us via our spirit, and we have our minds, but in the mind area we have thoughts coming from more than one source, so we can't just accept every thought that drifts into our minds, but we must examine them in light of God's Word, and only then are we to receive that thought.

> Romans 12:12; *"And be not conformed to this world: but be ye transformed by the <u>renewing of your mind</u>, that ye may prove what is that <u>good, and acceptable, and perfect</u>, will of God."*

See as a Christian we learn to discern between the two sources of thoughts. We have to cast down the evil thoughts, while receiving the good thoughts of God. In Heaven we can flow in the highest level of communicating by just receiving from God and flow with Him. Jesse in speaking with Jesus, had a thought (questions) would come into his mind, and before Jesse could speak it, Jesus would answer him. [5]

Dean Braxton Gets a Glimpse of Heaven

On August 6, 2012, Dean Braxton recalls, "He couldn't catch his breath. It was getting shallower and shallower, and he can remember saying to himself, "I am dying." He was in heaven. This time he saw Jesus. "The first thing that comes to him is, He's bright, just like John said, 'He's brighter than the noon day sun.' and the next phrase he say, he wish people could grab it, and it's this one, and 'He could look at Him.' And what you're looking at is not so much the physical part of Jesus; you're really experiencing the love He has for us. He tells people, 'It's like He only loves you and no one else.' Dean saw Him communicating to angels He would just look at them. Communication there was thought to thought. They would acknowledge receiving His information, bow before Him and then, back out."[17]

A Rodeo Cowboy's Freddy Vest Fight to Survive

On July 28th, 2008 Freddy was headed to a calf roping in Graham, Texas. By one o'clock that afternoon Freddy had made three successful calf roping runs. He was waiting to make his fourth when he suddenly dropped dead in the saddle. His friend, Dennis McKinley recalls that day: "He saw all this movement out of my left eye.

Then Dennis heard a real kind of a loud smack, and he looked and Freddy was on the ground. Dennis jumped off the fence, and he was the first one to Freddy. Dennis put his hand under his head and lifted it up and started praying for him." Freddy also remembers having conversations with God. "When he was there, there was communication, but the communication was inside of Freddy and it was nothing that verbally you would have ears to hear or a mouth to speak it."[18]

Heavenly Transportation

The means by which Roberts Liardon traveled to Heaven is that he was *flying through the heavens* at an incredible rate of speed. In a matter of a few moments, he landed on a flat space no larger than the average living room floor, outside an enormous gate, the biggest that he had ever seen. [6]

Marietta Davis, a 25-year-old American woman, living in Berlin, New York, fell into a trance for nine days during the summer of 1848 when she visit Heaven. [10]

Jesse Duplantis, suddenly felt a suction as if he was being pulled up out of his room. He heard a sound, whoosh! He was zooming along at a phenomenal rate of speed, being carried in something like a cable car. It was a chariot without a horse, but not like one of that you see in the movies, it was completely closed in.

Jesse said, "He could see through the windows that the chariot was racing along, but he had no idea how it was being operated.

Then he looked up, and there stood an angel and Jesse noted that it was the blonde-headed angel who had visited him before. The angel smiled and said, "You have an appointment with the Lord God Jehovah." Jesse said, "He felt the chariot slowing down; then it came to a stop. When the door opened, he experienced the shock of his life: he was in Heaven. As he moved closer toward the Holy City, toward God's Throne, he noticed trees were lined up alongside the River of life as it flowed throughout Paradise. Thousands of People were standing around under the trees. They all had been brought there in those chariot-like vehicles that he was brought in.[5]

Choo Thomas in her book "Heaven Is So Real" she states that she had many visits from Jesus who would come to meet her, after Jesus met her they would walk to right side of a hill that was alive with foliage. Choo Thomas could see a narrow, winding road snaking its way to the summit. Then they walked alongside a narrow river that flowed with the most crystal clear water Choo Thomas had ever seen. Jesus and Choo Thomas followed the river to the entrance of a shiny tunnel that seemed endless. Choo Thomas reasoned in herself that this must be the tunnel that people who had near-death experiences frequently described as the passageway from this life to the next. It was high and wide and, in comparison, the Lord and Choo Thomas were quite tiny. They walked through the mysterious tunnel, and when they emerged on the other side, they walked down to the beach again. The Lord said, "We are going to Heaven.

Then Jesus took the hand of Choo Thomas and they began to be lifted above the surface of the beach. They were literally flying through the air. They landed at a location that was filled with trees and grass, and their feet set down on a narrow, winding road, and from there they flew to Heaven.[3]

Mary K. Baxter, stated in her book *"A Divine Revelation of Heaven"* that she was transported to Heaven on many different occasion similar to that of Choo Thomas. [4]

Dr. Gary Wood was involved a car accident, and his spirit stepped outside of his body and He was in a swirling, funnel shape cloud that grew wider and wider and brighter and brighter. As he began to ascend up through this tunnel of light, he felt such a tranquil feeling of peace wash over him, wave after glorious wave. At the end of the brilliant tunnel was a pathway he revealed that "He could see down the path a very bright, yet not blinding light. He could hear the angel singing all around him", "Worthy is the Lamb that was slain to receive glory, Power, wisdom, and dominion be Thine forever, oh Lord, amen and amen. He saw the cloud open up wide and began walking on green grass. [2]

Chapter 16
Heavenly Creative Inventions

Proverbs 8:12 *"I wisdom dwell with prudence, and find out knowledge of witty inventions."*

Shawn Bolz, in his book the Keys to Heaven's Economy, *An Angelic Visitation* from Minister of Finance shares how in 1997. He was transported to a heavenly realm and taken to a huge warehouse. He states that he could not distinguish the ceiling or walls even though the room was enclosed. The angel who oversaw the storehouse was assigned to show him around. As he was taken on a tour through different sections of the building, he was gripped by anticipation. "What is this place?" Shawn asked. His eyes lit up. The Angel smiled and replied, "This is the storehouse of Heaven."

After this, Shawn was quickly carried away by the Spirit to a different section called Creative Inventions. Although it was a vest area, it seemed that each place they entered became larger.

Lights and colors swirled around, and the Holy Spirit seemed to hover and flash like lighting. Somehow Shawn knew the Holy Spirit had visited many people in their minds and imaginations with the same flashes that he was witnessing in Heaven. Shawn was sparked by the capacity to invent and create what he was viewing in this storehouse. Each type of technology was represented there: agricultural, computer science, medical. Many cures for diseases were in this section.

Toys were there, sound devices, video and multimedia machines - so many basic materials already known to create revolutionary advancements for the earth. The Spirit of Revelation would have to reveal the various combinations. Angels guarded certain inventions. Shawn tried to discern why guards existed in this area, and then He noticed some people trying to gain illegal access through witchcraft to steal these inventions.

An example of this was revealed to Shawn, in a vision, Shawn saw God send an angel to the earth and offer a Christian the invention to steward an invention. The man began to create the invention, but he ran into trouble with his finances and relationships because of the warfare surrounding the project. Instead of interceding and beseeching God for provision and protection, the man remained immersed in his work and closed his heart to Heaven.

During this time, a very wealthy man was sent by a demonic force to meet this Christian. The wealthy man offered to fund the man's invention, the Christian peremptorily agreed to this, but later when they sealed the deal, the wealthy man stole the technology and since has manipulated the business deal in his favor. Because he had lost faith in Heaven's provision and God's faithfulness, the Christian had been so desperate and rash that he would have said yes to almost any contract. So the enemy stole and won the use of a precious, divinely inspired communication system, which satan had used to defile humanity all over the globe with every form of perversion. After this, Shawn understood why guardians watch over this and other areas of the heavenly storehouse. [9]

Section II

Horror beneath the Grave

"**Hell from beneath** is moved for thee to meet thee at thy coming: it stirreth up the dead for thee, even all the chief ones of the earth; it hath raised up from their thrones all the kings of the nations." *Isaiah 14:9*

Chapter 17
Hell and its location

Isaiah 14:9 *"Hell from beneath is moved for thee to meet thee at thy coming: it stirreth up the dead for thee, even all the chief ones of the earth; it hath raised up from their thrones all the kings of the nations."*

Introduction

In our endeavor to share with you about Hell and its location we must understand that there are underground chambers. In the Bible there are five word different words that are used to identify what we call the underworld, at times when we use the word Hell, and we think that is an all exclusive word to cover what's going to happen to the devil and his cohorts. As we read *Matthew 25:41*; "Then shall he say also unto them on the left hand, Depart from me, ye cursed, into everlasting fire, prepared for the devil and his angels:"

Something mysterious and unknown "ages past" of *Genesis 1:1* and the fall of satan in *Genesis 1:2*, the expulsion of satan from the heaven to earth must have caused some type on tremendous impact on the earth when satan failed like lightning based on *Luke 10:18*. Some have suggested, that this was the time that God created the place called hell in the heart of the earth. It is clear that hell was never created for man, but was originally intended only for satan and his rebellious angels.

In the Bible there are five words that we need to understand if we truly want to understand Hell and its location.

These words are:

Sheol - a Hebrew Old Testament word
Hades - a Greek New Testament word
Gehenna - a Greek New Testament word
Tartarus - a Greek New Testament word
Abyss - a Greek New Testament word

The first word *Sheol* is used sixty-five times in the Old Testament. It is translated as hell in the Bible, thirty-one times in the Bible, thirty-one times as "grave," and three times as "pit."

The second word *Hades* is translated as hell ten times in the New Testament. In *1st Corinthians 15:55*: "O death, where *is* thy sting? O grave, where *is* thy victory?" Will it translate to the grave? In *Revelation 6:8*, death is identified as the rider of a pale horse, and hell (Hades) follows him. By definition the word Hades is "the region of departed spirits of the lost (but including the blessed dead in periods preceding the ascension of Christ)."[3]

The third word *Geenna* translated Gehenna is found eleven times in the four Gospel (Matthew, Mark, Luke and John) as "hell."

The fourth word *Tartarus* - is a Greek word translated as "hell" is found in only two places:

"For if God spared not the angels that sinned, but cast them down to hell, and delivered them into chains of darkness, to be reserved unto judgment;" (2 Peter 2:4)

Jude 1:6; "And the angels which kept not their first estate, but left their own habitation, he hath reserved in everlasting chains under darkness unto the judgment of the great day"

Tartarus was considered both as spirit or a deity in Greek mythology and the place of a chamber lower than Hades in which the most wicked spirits confined.

It was believed to be the first place created in the regions of the underworld, as angels fell into sin age before Adam was created and sinned. Peter and Jude reveal that this is the chamber of fallen angels.

The final word revealing another chamber under the earth is the Greek Abusso, which is translated in English – as the word *abyss*. This word is found nine times in the New Testament and is translated in the Book of Revelation as "bottomless pit" (*Revelation 9:1-2; 11; 11:7; 17:8; 20:1, 3*). This place was known to the evil spirits, Christ encountered during His ministry. On one occasion, Christ expelled a large host of demons from a man, and the chief evil spirit requested not to be confined in the "deep" (*Luke 8:31*).

These words – Sheol, Hades, Gehenna, Tartarus, and the abyss are the five main words used to identify the underground world of fallen angels, certain evil spirits, and the souls of the unrighteous.

The Location of the Underground Chambers

First, these chambers and caverns are all located underneath the earth's surface. In the Scriptures, heaven is always identified as being up, and hell is always referred to as being down or beneath:

Number 16:30 *"But if the LORD make a new thing, and the earth open her mouth, and swallow them up, with all that appertain unto them, and they go down quick into the pit; then ye shall understand that these men have provoked the LORD."*

Job 11:8 *"It is as high as heaven; what canst thou do? deeper than hell; what canst thou now?"*

Isaiah 14:9 *"Hell from beneath is moved for thee to meet thee at thy coming: it stirreth up the dead for thee, even all the chief ones of the earth; it hath raised up from their thrones all the kings of the nations."*

Never is hell spoken of as being up, and never is heaven's location given as down. Second, these underground holding places for the unrighteous and fallen angels are under mountains, as revealed in the story of Jonah. Jonah 2:6

"And many entrances are located under the seas." Job 26:5.

Hell is definitely located down and under the earth:

- "go down quick into hell" Psalms 55:15
- "shalt be brought down to hell" Isaiah 14:15
- "cast him down to hell" Ezekiel 31:16
- "They also went down into hell" Ezekiel 31:17
- "God spared not the angels that sinned, but cast them down to hell" 2 Peter 2:4

One example of hell under the crust of the earth is in the case of the rebellion of Korah against Moses. Korah was jealous of Moses' and Aaron's authority over the people and sought to lead a coup against these men of God. God brought a sudden judgment on Korah and his rebels:

> Number 16:32; *"And the earth opened her mouth, and swallowed them up, and their houses, and all the men that appertained unto Korah, and all their goods."*

Testimony of other concerning the location of Hell:

Mary K. Baxter states "To those of you, who think hell is here on earth well, you are right – it is! Hell is in the center of the earth, and there are souls in torment there night and day. There are no parties in hell. No love. No compassion. No rest, only a place of sorrow beyond your belief." [11]

Bill Wiese ascended thru a tunnel to the surface. He had been in the center of the earth "As the Lord and Bill were having this time together, they kept ascending up the tunnel. They came to the earth's surface, and then they continued upward. They went high above the earth until we were out of the atmosphere."[12]

Hell is in center of Earth 3700 mile deep "Bill believes the scripture states that presently it is in the center of the earth. He has listed some of the verses below. Note that somehow he knew that it was in the lower part of the earth, and he sensed it to dwell down thirty seven hundred miles deep.

It was as if my senses were keener or more aware than usual." ... "I remember falling to get there and ascending through the tunnel when he left." [12]

Dr. Roger Mills, say... "Then the Lord said to me, "I have to take you on a tour through the Outer Darkness of Hell..." As he heard God say that to him, just then... at that very moment, he remembers the sensation of flying upwards into what appeared to be outer space. He remember the sensation of floating out into the darkness of deep space, first upward toward the sky, then slowly descending into black darkness until he was not able to see anything. "His surroundings reminded him of an underground coalmine. The ground was made of black rock, the walls were the same, and the atmosphere that he was in was very dark." (Implied under the earth) [13]

Chapter 18
The Entrance to Hell and (Portals to Hell)

Mary K. Baxter states "Soon we were high into the heavens." "They began to go even higher into the sky, and now she could see the earth below. Protruding out of the earth and scattered about in many places were funnels spinning around to a center point and then turning back again. These moved high above the earth and looked like a giant, dirty type of slinky that moved continuously. They were coming up from all over the earth. "What are these?" She asked the Lord Jesus and they came near to one." "These are the gateways to hell, He said. "We will go into hell through one of them." [11]

Dr. Roger Mills shared… "Roads/pathways to hell are imbedded in Earth and protrude to outer space. Those who refuse God are sucked in when they die.

"The Outer Darkness of Hell has many tunnel-like pathways within it, which he describes as corridors. They are long, circular and black, and they stretch from the Earth to outer space, into the Outer Darkness of Hell. The look like beams of long black clouds stretched all throughout the Earth and outer space. These long, dirty, black clouds, which look to me like corridors or tunnels…God, told him he has named them pathways or the roads to Hell. [13]

Matthew 7:13-14 NLT *"You can enter God's Kingdom only through the narrow gate. The highway to Hell is broad, and it's gate is wide for the many who choose the easy way. But the gateway to life is small, and the road is narrow, and only a few ever find it.*

He also said that these pathways or roads to Hell work much like a vacuum pump with a powerful suction pull. Jesus explained to Dr. Roger Mills that they are embedded in the Earth by the thousands, protruding up through Earth's atmosphere into outer space. God explained to Dr. Roger Mills that if a person refuses to accept Him as their Almighty God and they have no intention of repenting of their sins, then whenever he or she dies their human soul and spirit are immediately sucked up through one of these long, black clouds, which will lead them into the Outer Darkness of Hell."

Chapter 19
Cells, Pits, and Rooms of Hell

Isaiah 14:15-17 *"Yet thou shalt be brought down to hell, to the sides of the pit. [16] They that see thee shall narrowly look upon thee, and consider thee, saying, Is this the man that made the earth to tremble, that did shake kingdoms; [17] That made the world as a wilderness, and destroyed the cities thereof; that opened not the house of his prisoners?"*

Mary K. Baxter states "There were pits of fire everywhere as far as the eye could see. The pits were four feet across and three feet deep and shaped like a bowl."

"Brimstone was embedded in the side of the pit and glowed red like hot coals of a fire." In belly of hell (witchcraft, sorcery, drug peddlers idol worshipers) [11]

"Jesus and Mary K. Baxter stood on a ledge at the first tier of cells." "Beside the ledge, or walkway, were the cells that had been dug into the earth. Like jail cells, these calls were all in a row, with only two feet of dirt separating them." "Jesus said "This cell block is seventeen mils high, starting from the bottom of hell. Here in these cells are many souls that were in witchcraft or the occult. Some were sorcerers, mediums, drug peddlers, idol worshippers or evil people with familiar spirits."[11]

Bill Wiese stated…"Cell with bars, complete darkness attacked by many demons; at his point of arrival was a cell that was approximately fifteen feet high by ten feet wide with a fifteen foot depth. With its walls of rough stone and rigid bars on the door, he felt as though he was in a temporary holding area." [12]

Even if people are in the same pit, their suffering is personal, there is no companionship. "Now it is true that there are areas in this vast, fiery pit where people are thrown together, but they are only *together* in the sense that they are all experiencing the same torment. Each person is very isolated in extreme agony and screaming in fear as fire and brimstone rain down upon them. They are *together* in the same way cattle are herded into a slaughter house. A soul in such extreme agony would have no opportunity for a conversation." [12]

"To the right of the large inferno were thousands of small pits, as far as I could see. Each pit was no more than three to five feet across and four to five feet deep – each pit holding a single lost soul."[12]

Dr. Roger Mills shared… Each Individual pit is made for a specific person, so they vary in size. "He almost walked into what looked like a bit manhole. God said to me, "The hole you were about to walk into is a pit. There are many pits in this area of Hades [Hell].

Some of these outs are big and some are small"….While staring at the particular pit he was about to walk into, God explained to him that it was four feet wide all around, and six feet deep. He told him that there are different pit sizes. They are custom made to fit the physical and spiritual dimensions of the damned."[13]

Room of Dead Faith - Things prayed for but not in faith. "Jesus and Dr. Roger Mills were still on Outer Darkness. They were standing in front of the door that is called *Room of Dead Faith*. Behind this door is a room. It was created to house the faithless prayers and desires of the righteous."… When Roger looked in the door he saw a microwave oven, and he asked God in amazement, "What is a microwave oven doing in Hell?" Still looking at the room, he began to see all types of furniture, cars, houses and other household appliances. "This is too weird," he thought. Then he saw men's, women's and children's clothing, all with the price tags still on them. he saw human body parts… limbs such as arms and legs. He became perplexed over what he was seeing in the room. God knew Roger was confused about the Room of Dead Faith…. God said unto him, "Look, listen and learn. The things you saw in that room are the many things that belong too many of my people who are alive on the Earth today. They have been praying and asking me to give them certain things, but they are praying with the wrong attitude. Most of my children ask me for things, but they do not believe that I will give them what they ask. In other words, they have no Faith.[13]

Room of Dead Works – Many works done but little fruit, (Re: a certain church) "Though her works seem many, they are all very dead. Tell her Jesus said repent or He will come in judgment against her very quickly.

Room of the cursed - God moved the trees of Eden to a room in hell except the Tree of Life – HE is the Tree of Life.

"Once again God paused for a moment. Roger watched tears begin to form in his eyes, and he said to me, "Roger, I have always used trees as a symbol to describe people."[13]

John 15:5 *"I am the Vine, and ye are the branches: He that abideth in me, and I in him, the same bringeth forth much fruit; for without me ye can do nothing"*

Room of Sin - Woman's beauty represents sin. Sin infects us at birth. "The Lord God-Jesus looked into my eyes and said, "Roger I know that you thought you had met this woman back upon the Earth. A woman she is not, but yes you have met her, as have all creation. Her spirit was there, rejoicing at your birth. The day you were born, her spirit infected your soul. Every human soul at the time of birth was infected by her."[13]

The Earth was bound by Sin's power. That is why I came into the world, that I might destroy the power of sin." All have sin because Adam infected them. It's not their fault. Jesus died to give us clean DNA. [13]

"The Lord God-Jesus went on to explain, "… When Adam sinned, sin entered the entire human race. Adam's disobedience to the command I gave him in the garden was sin. His sin brought death on him and the entire human race. Every person that has ever been born, he or she enters into this world as a sinner, not because of what they did, but as a result of what Adam did. When I died on the cross centuries ago, my blood was spilled that I might give everyone that would believe in me a clean bloodstream and pure DNA, thus making everyone that would accept me free from Sin. Sin has no power over us unless we allow and wallow in it."[13]

"The Lord God-Jesus continued to say, "I have literally imprisoned the spiritual powers of Sin. Although Sin is defeated and bound, men still have free will to engross themselves in Sin, but it is not because of the spiritual powers of Sin. [13]

Cold side of hell! Sexual misconduct, thievery from the poor and not repenting, then the Lord God-Jesus looked at Roger and said, "…Woe is unto anyone who causes hurt, pain and corruption for little children. Roger, this man was a business man in San Francisco, California. He made a lot of money by soliciting pornographic material of children. He had plenty of time to repent, but he wouldn't. [13]

Chapter 20
Creatures of Hell

Mary K. Baxter says…"Along the sides of this tunnel were living forms embedded in the walls. Dark gray in color, the forms moved and cried out to us as we passed. She knew without being told that they were evil. The forms could move but were still attached to the walls. A horrible smell came from them, and they screeched at us with the most awful cries. I felt an invisible, evil force moving inside those tunnels.

At times in the darkness, Mary could make out the forms. A dirty fog covered most of them. "Lord, what are these?" she asked as she held tightly onto Jesus' hand. He said, "These are evil spirits ready to be spewed out on the earth when satan gives the orders." (Foggy forms) [11] "As she continued to look, she saw those ugly snakes were slithering about everywhere." (Snakes) [11]

She thought she was going to get out when a large demon with great wings that seemed broken at the top and hung down his sides ran to her. His color was brownish-black, and he had hair all over is large form. His eyes were set far back in his head, and he was about the size of a large grizzly bear." (Large winged demon) [11]

The one speaking was very large, about the size of a full grown grizzly bear, brown in color, with a head like a bat and eyes that were set very far back into a hairy face. Hairy arms fell to his sides, and fangs came out of the hair on his face.

Another one was small like a monkey with very long arms and with hair all over his body. His face was tiny, and he had a pointed nose. Mary could see no eyes on him anywhere. Still another had a large head, large ears and a long tail, while yet one more was as large as a horse and had smooth skin." (Imps and other demons of varying size) "…Mary began to see great snakes, large rats and many evil spirits, all running form the presence of the Lord. "[11]

Imps and devils were all over the sides of this cavern and they were all going somewhere up and out of the tunnel. In front of us, sitting on a hill, was a large woman. She was swaying back and forth as though she was drunk. Written on her were the words "Mystery Babylon." Mary know knew the mother of all abominations on the earth came from hell. An evil powerful force emanated from her…" woman - Mystery Babylon"[11]

Bill Wiese stated… "The walls wrapped around me and led to the vast expanse of the pit. As he looked at the walls, he saw that they were covered with thousands of hideous creatures. These demonic creatures were all sizes and shapes. Some of them had four legs and were the size of bears. Others stood upright and were about the size of gorillas. They were all terribly grotesque and disfigured. It looked as if their flesh had been decomposing and all their limbs were twisted and out of proportion. Some displayed immense long arms or abnormally large feet. They seemed to me to be the living dead." [12]

There were also gigantic rats and huge spiders at least two feet wide and two to three feet high. Bill also saw snakes and worms, ranging from small to enormously large. Bill was petrified and could not believe his eyes. His gaze followed the beasts up the sides of the cell, and he saw that there was a hole in the top of the cave. It was the entrance to the upward tunnel, approximately thirty-five feet in diameter. The fiendish creatures lined the tunnel walls as well. They were distinctly wicked. Their eyes were cauldrons of evil and death. Everything was filth, stinking, rotten, and foul. There was one other disgusting aspect about these creatures they all seemed to possess a hatred for mankind. They were the epitome of evil. "The creatures seemed to be chained, or attached in some fashion, to the cavern walls. Bill was relieved to know they could not reach him." [12]

"Some people have asked Bill, "Does the Bible support demons that are twelve to thirteen feet tall?" In a tape series by Chuck Missler, he gives an explanation for the height of some of the demons he saw in hell. He speaks of the portion of the book of Genesis that describes "giants on the earth" which came about as the result of the fallen angels that slept with women and bore children who were called "might men" Genesis 6:2-4.

He also refers to Jude, which talks about angels (fallen) who didn't stay in their proper domain, but who left their abode and gave themselves over to sexual immorality"

The remnants of the giants is mentioned in Deuteronomy 3:11, where it specifically calls out a man whose iron bed was approximately 13 ½ feet long." It is reasonable to conclude that the unusually large size of men was a direct result of contact with the fallen angels. The fallen angels themselves where probably very large, these evil angels were cast down to hell as mentioned in Jude 6-7 and 2 Peter 2:4. [1]

The Bible indicates that demons have enormous strength. Bill say that he can tell from his experience that they exhibited great strength with him. They picked him up as if he weighed nothing. He had a sense that they were a thousand times stronger than the strength of a normal man. Please examine the verses yourself.

> Psalm 103:20 *"His angels, who excel in strength"*

> Matthew 8;28; *"Two demon-possessed an exceedingly fierce, so that no one could pass that way"*

> Mark 5:2-4 *there met Him… a man with an unclean spirit and no one could bind him, not even with chains, because he had often been bound with shackles and chains. And the chains had been pulled apart by him, and the shackles broken in pieces, neither could anyone tame him.*

> 2 Peter 2:11 *Angels, who are great in power and might"*

There may be some differences in fallen angels and demons, but that is another topic. Both demons and angels (not fallen angels, but angels in general) are addressed in the above verses, both exhibiting great strength. Therefore, it seems reasonable to conclude that it would be possible that demons in hell, or fallen angels, would have great strength also.

Dr. Roger Mills said… "Tiny black spiders with red eyes and teeth, biting denizens, he saw a huge show racing across the ground. As the shadow came closer to where the Lord God-Jesus and he were standing, he got a closer look at it and he realized that he was not looking at a shadow.

It was thousands of tiny black spiders…. he noticed they had teeth and eyes. He watched as they entered the jail cells, and began to crawl all over the bishops, attacking and biting them all over with their teeth. …thousands of black spiders covered them like a blanket. [13]

Chapter 21
The place of Outer Darkness

Matthew 8:12 *"But the children of the kingdom shall be cast **out** into **outer darkness**: there shall be weeping and gnashing of teeth.*

Mary K. Baxter states that Outer Darkness is "A place of darkness thrown by a demon, for those who were saved but backslid. "As they walked on through hell, Jesus and Mary came upon a very large and very dark man. He was enshrouded in darkness and had the appearance of an angel. He was holding something in his left hand." [11]

Jesus said, *"This place is called outer darkness."I heard weeping and gnashing of teeth.*

The only light was from the fire the lost souls were swimming in. Nowhere before had there been such utter hopelessness as she felt in this place. The angel that stood before us had no wings. He looked to be about thirty feet tall, and he knew exactly what he was doing. He had a large disk in his left hand and was turning slowly with this disk lifted up high as though he was getting ready to throw it. There was a fire in the middle of the disk, and blackness on the outer edge. The angel held his hand beneath the disk and reached far back in order to get more leverage. Mary wondered who this angel was and what he was about to do." [11]

Jesus knew her thoughts and said again, "This is the outer darkness. Remember that my Word says,

The children of the kingdom shall be cast out into the outer darkness; there shall be weeping and gnashing of teeth."

"Lord," she said, "You mean your servants are here?" "Yes, "said Jesus, "servants that turned back after I called them. Servants who loves the world more than Me and went back to wallowing in more sin. Servants that would not stand for the truth and for holiness, it is better that one never starts than to turn back after the beginning to serve Me."

"I watched the dark angel as he cast the large disk far, far out into the darkness. And then, immediately, Jesus and I were in the air following this disk through space. We came to the outside of the disk and stood looking in. There was a fire in the center of the disk, and people were swimming in and out, over and under the flaming waves. There were no demons or evil spirits here, only souls burning in a sea of fire.

Outside the disk was the blackest of darkness. Only the light from the Flames in the disk illuminated the night air. In that light Mary saw people trying to swim to the edges of the disk. Some of them would almost reach the sides when a suction force from inside the disk would drag them back into the flames. Mary watched as their forms turned to skeletons with misty-gray souls. Mary knew then that this was just another part of hell." [11]

Dr. Roger Mills also saw "The outer darkness is reserved for those who willfully reject Jesus. The Lord God-Jesus continued to say, "It was never my intention to send any living human to Hell. Listen, look and learn. I never send anyone to Hell. They send themselves.

On Earth, when men and women refuse to accept my Holy Word, and refuse to have me in their lives, with that attitude, after death there is only one place that they can come, and that is down here to Hell." [13]

Chapter 22
Types of Torment in Hell

Luke 16:19-24 *a certain rich man, which was clothed in purple and fine linen, and fared sumptuously every day: [20] And there was a certain beggar named Lazarus, which was laid at his gate, full of sores, [21] And desiring to be fed with the crumbs which fell from the rich man's table: moreover the dogs came and licked his sores. [22] And it came to pass, that the beggar died, and was carried by the angels into Abraham's bosom: the rich man also died, and was buried; [23] And in hell he lift up his eyes, being in torments, and seeth Abraham afar off, and Lazarus in his bosom. [24] And he cried and said, Father Abraham, have mercy on me, and send Lazarus that he may dip the tip of his finger in water, and cool my tongue; for I am tormented in this flame.*

Mary K. Baxter said that she saw, "Fire and worms on grey skeleton and decayed flesh. The skeleton formed the shape of a woman was a dirty-grey mist inside was talking to Jesus. In shock, she listened to her. Decayed flesh hung by shreds from her bones, and, as it burned, it fell off into the bottom of the pit. Where her eyes had once been were now only empty sockets. She had no hair. The fire started at her feet in small flames and grew as it climbed up and over her body. The woman seemed to be constantly burning, even when the flames were only embers. From deep down inside came her cries and groans of despair, "Lord, Lord, I want out of here!" [11]

Mary K. looked at the woman again, and worms were crawling out of the bones of her skeleton. They were not harmed by the fire. Jesus said, "She knows and feels those worms inside." [11]

(Fun center – people taken to be tortured, those who served satan wholeheartedly are tortured by those deceived). "Jesus told Mary K. that there is a place in hell called the "fun center." Souls confined to the pits cannot be brought there. He also told Mary K. that though torments are different for different souls, all are burned by fire. The fun center is shaped like a circus arena.

Several people who are to be the entertainment are brought to the center ring of the fun center. These are people who knowingly served Satan on earth. They are the ones who, of their own free will, chose to follow Satan instead of God. Around the sides of the arena are the other souls, except those in the pits."

"The ones who had been deceived and were caused to fall into sin came and tortured their deceivers. One by one they were allowed to torture them." [11]

Souls torn apart and used as scavenger hunts; great pain, "In one such torment, spiritual bones were taken apart and buried in different parts of hell. The soul was literally torn apart and the parts scattered across hell in a kind of demonic scavenger hunt. The mutilated souls felt tremendous pain. Those outside the arena could throw stones at those who were in the arena. Every imaginable method of torture was allowed." [11]

Dr. Roger Mills says… "Worm attached to spine torments racist priest "…I am a preacher too, and I am here because I was preaching hate, and I was prejudiced. I used to do pastoral work at a church in downtown Detroit, named St. Mary's Catholic Church. I was a practicing priest there during the 1960s.

She was there during the 60's riots and I did not like any of the black parishioners that walked through the church door. I was a racist, and in my opinion thought I was doing God a favor by hating and being prejudiced toward anyone who was not of my race....God appeared to me here in Hell, and he told me that I was here because I judged my black brothers and sisters and that I had hate in my heart."[13]

> John 15:12 *"This is my commandment, That ye love one another, as I have loved you."*

Dr. Mills continued to watch this pitiful soul as he began to grab the left side of his rib cage, which displayed a thin layer of skin. When he moved his hand Dr. Mills saw the longed worm that he has ever seen. Dr. Mills thought it was a snake. "The worm was white; somewhat like an albino in appearance. He watched as the work unwrapped itself from the back of the man's spine. It almost camouflaged itself; the worm took on the same appearance of the skeleton, and he would never have known it was there, because he did not see it until it moved. The worm was about five to six feet long. He watched as it crawled its way from the right side of his ribcage, sliding through his skeleton-stomach area, to the left side of his ribcage, he watched as the worm began to eat its way through the remaining skin on the left side of the ribcage, and he heard the man scream in horror and great pain." [13]

Maurice S. Rawlings, M.D. talks about the "Black and heavy pressure, dry heat, parched tongue, eyes feel like coals, breathing feels like blast form a furnace."[15]

In 1948, for example, George Godwin of Alberta, Canada related a despairing near-death affair…"He was guided to a place in the spirit world called Hell. This was a place of punishment for all those who reject Jesus Christ.

He not only saw Hell, but felt the torment that all who goes there will experience. The darkness of Hell is so intense that is seems to have pressure per square inch.

It is an extremely black, dismal, desolate, heavy, pressurized type of darkness. It gives the individual a crushing, despondent feeling of loneliness.

The heat is a dry, debilitating type. Your eyeballs are so dry they feel like red hot coals in their sockets. Your tongue and lips are parched and cracked with the intense heat. The breath from your nostrils as well as the air you breathe feels like a blast from a furnace. The exterior of your body feels as though it were encased within a white hot stove. The interior of your body has a sensation of scorching air being forced through it. The agony and loneliness cannot be properly expressed clearly enough for proper understanding to the human soul; it has to be experienced. [15]

Chapter 23
Hell Invention and activities of Hell

Jesus said "My child, He said, "God, our Father, give each of us a will so that we could choose whether we would serve Him or satan. See, God did not make hell for His people. satan deceives many into following him, but hell was made for satan and his angels. It is not Jesus desire, not that of My Father, that anyone should perish."

"It was never God's intention to send anyone to hell they send themselves" The Lord God-Jesus continued to say, "It was never my intention to send any living human to Hell. Listen, look and learn. He never send anyone to Hell. They send themselves. On Earth, when men and women refuse to accept my Holy Word, and refuse to have me in their lives, with that attitude, after death there is only one place that they can come, and that is down here to Hell." Hell was created for satan and his demons, then the Lord God Jesus looked at me, smiled, and said, "…Just as He created the Lake of Fire for the Devil and his angels, the Bottomless Pit as well was created for the Devil and his angels."[13]

The Activity of Hell

"The demons that are there as result of fallen angels mating with women want to inhabit people. satan and his high-ranking demons have thrones on 1st level of heaven (Earth), the 2nd level of heaven (the heavens/sky)." [13]

The angels that sexually sinned with the women of the Earth before Noah's flood, there are not demonic spirits. They are fallen angels.

The demon spirits that are now roaming the Earth in your day and time are the offspring of those fallen angels who did have sexual intercourse with some on the women of the earth (See Genesis 6:1-2 and 4.)

Rather, demon spirits are the spirits of the giants because they were part human and part angelic in nature, whenever the giants died, and their spirits left their bodies and bared the appearance of animal-like creatures....These demons spend most of their time fighting against the human race on Earth. [13]

Excerpt from Ricarado Cid eight hours in Heaven

Ricarado Cid after finishing a time of intercession, he came later one night for a church service. After the bishop's benediction, He lifted up his hands and felt someone pass by and touch his back. When this happened, he lost all strength and fell to the floor. The bishop asked what was wrong with him and Ricarado responded he don't know, He had no strength and he could hardly talk. Then the church surrounded him and began to pray in tongues and shout. Then some of the congregation could see the angel that was coming in and asking Ricarado to leave his body. The bishop declared, *"You will not leave your body!"* As he said this, the angel stopped motioning for Ricarado to leave his body. You see, any person who has authority in Jesus will be honored by the angel of the Lord. The bishop then asked him, *"How long does the angel want to take you from your body?"* Ricarado then asked the angel, *"Are you taking me for one hour? Two? Three hours?"* The angel replied, *"No, you will be gone for 8 hours to see Jesus in the third heaven because He wants to talk to you."*

Then, the angel told Ricarado, *"I am not the one who will escort you to heaven, because I am your guardian angel who has protected you every day you have lived on this earth. Two angels will come from heaven to take you to the third heaven at the midnight hour."*

Ricarado told this to the bishop and he determined to take Ricarado in another brother's car to a pastor's home on a second floor. As Ricarado lay in a room, they were able to hear dogs barking and people screaming. After Ricarado experience, he was told that two men in bright white shining robes appeared in the middle of the street and walked into the first floor of the building and came up to the second floor where he was staying. *These angels were beautiful. They had brilliant white hair, whiter than snow and eyes that were fashioned like pearls. Their skin was as soft as a baby's yet their bodies were muscular like a bodybuilder. These angels are powerful!! Ricarado then told the bishop, these angels are here that were sent to take me to heaven. One of the angels started motioning Ricarado to leave his body.*

As this happened, his bones started hurting again. So, the brothers in Christ next to him and started massaging his body and telling him that he was getting ice cold. Next, they went to get portable heaters to heat my body up again. As the angels were calling him to leave his body, he started to get desperate and moving from one side to the other. He started feeling death take over his body and he shouted to his brothers in Christ, "Don't bury me, I will be back!" Ricarado left his body, and then Ricarado jumped on his bed. Ricarado saw his brothers in Christ touching his body and saying, *"He's gone, he left his body!"* But Ricarado was right there next to them telling them, *"He was there!"*

However, they couldn't see Ricarado body because it was an incorruptible spirit body. His brothers started wrapping my body in a blanket.

One of the angels told Ricarado, *"It's time to go, because the Lord is waiting for you!"* Each angel took him by an arm and lifted him up to the heavens and they crossed through the <u>atmosphere at lightning speed</u>. Ricarado said, he will tell you this, even if you don't believe any of this, my Jesus Christ exists and lives forever!

As Ricarado left his body that night they were flying at an incredible rate of speed on their way to visit the Lord. Ricarado was able to look down and see the planet earth. Then they passed right next to the moon, this glorious moon that brightens the night sky on the earth. Then, Ricarado was able to see the giant sun with his own eyes; he was able to see the flames that explode from the sun and warm the earth. Then they continued on and Ricarado saw many stars as he passed by them. God allowed Ricarado to see the sun, moon, and stars for a purpose: that purpose is to tell all of you that our God is a huge creator of the universe!!! He's not small by any means! They continued traveling at a great rate of speed until they reached a place where there were no more stars.

No more creation, just darkness. You could look down and see all of the stars below them. Ricarado started feeling afraid and asking the angels, *"Where are you taking me? Please take me back to my body on the earth!"* They angels squeezed Ricarado tight and wrapped one of each of their legs around his and held him.

Ricarado then started bending over in somewhat of a fetal position because of the fear he felt. The angels said *"Be quiet! We are taking you to the third heaven where Jesus is waiting to talk with you!"* The angels stopped and during this moment Ricarado was looking in all directions but couldn't see anything created, he didn't know where he was, but he thought this was the second heaven.

Ricarado then was bracing himself in a fetal position while the angels were holding him and suddenly he felt and heard the terrible noise of a stampede above me. The angels squeezed him and said, *"Ricardo, don't fear, Jesus is with us!"* As they were speaking, they also said, *"Turn up your head and look above you!"* Ricarado then was surprised by what he was looking at because there was some kind of motion by creatures above them. One of the angels said, *"Look, we will show you what you are looking at above us!"* And one of the angels motioned with his hand from one side to the other and illuminated the entire sky above us to see what was there. As the sky was illuminated there was nothing but demons and devils surrounding the entire sky. Ricarado asked the angel, *"What is this place?"* One of them responded, *"This is the celestial realm of darkness where Satan and his demons inhabit."*

Ricarado started saying, *"That's why there's so much evil on the earth! These demons come to the earth from this realm and cause all forms of destruction and wickedness on the race of men. The earth is full of demons!"* There are millions upon millions, the number is uncountable.

Then the angels started motioning for me to look more closely and they showed me the faces of these creatures and that many of these horrible beings are already shown to us on television.

These beings were MONSTROUS!! Ricarado saw the **Thundercats** and **Power Rangers** and **comic strips from animations and horror movies in real life**. All of the creators of these movies and **animations** have formed a pact with the devil to produce these things for television and cinema!! All of those drawings come from that spiritual realm that Ricarado experienced. Why do you think that nowadays children are so rebellious?? It's because those demons enter into your children as they view these shows that depict them. That's why we need to learn to teach our kids how to discern what to watch on TV.

The angel told Ricarado that this is all a reality and truth. All these demons exist and people are making pacts with the devil to bring these demons to the earth. These demons started to curse me, and the church, and the Father, and the Lord Jesus and the earth because they don't respect God or any his creation. Then, Ricarado saw in the flesh a goblin named **Hugo**, who is a popular cartoon caricature in Chile. He was horrifying to look at. He came near me and told me, *"they will go to the earth and kill all the children!"*

Why do you think that children are killing children? It's because some of them said that something came out of the television and told me to do this or that. These demons are planting hatred on the earth, may the Lord deliver and cleanse Chile!! [20]

Chapter 24
Bottomless Pit and Lake of Fire

Revelation 9:1-3 *"And the fifth angel sounded, and I saw a star fall from heaven unto the earth: and to him was given the key of the bottomless pit. ² And he opened the bottomless pit; and there arose a smoke out of the pit, as the smoke of a great furnace; and the sun and the air were darkened by reason of the smoke of the pit. ³ And there came out of the smoke locusts upon the earth: and unto them was given power, as the scorpions of the earth have power.* (Revelation 20:14-15)

The Bottomless Pit

Dr. Roger Mills states that The Lord God-Jesus said to him, "My peace is with you. I am with you; I am more than the world against you. So nothing by any means shall harm you." Then the Lord God-Jesus pointed at a big circular area that was about fifteen feet in front of us. We walked over and stood at the edge of the circular area. The big circle was the color of copper, it appeared to be a giant metal Lid, and written around the edge of the lid, in English, "The Bottomless Pit."

In the center of the lid was a handle, and attached to the handle was a big chain. The lid must have been half the size of a football field. In additional, on top of the lid there was something that resembled a keyhole. The entire pit was circular in shape. Just then the Lord God Jesus said to him, "Behold the Bottomless Pit!" He watched in amazement as the Lord God-Jesus grabbed a hold of the chain and inserted something into the hole in the lid that looked like a key.

Then He removed the lid. As He was moving it to uncover that huge hole, the screech and the noise from that lid sounded like animals howling.

When the lid was completely removed, there was a gust of wind coming out of the hole, which felt very much like a huge vacuum suction pump. Dr. Roger Mills was immediately sucked into the hole, and he screamed at the top of his voice to the Lord God-Jesus, "Help me! Help me!" He fell into what seemed to be a tornado or a funnel cloud. He began to twist and turn violently, and instantly he came to a stop. In mid-air…in darkness, the Lord God-Jesus appeared beside him and He said to "Roger, my peace I give you. I told you that I would never leave you, nor forsake you. I have chosen you for this very moment to reveal to you, in the outer Darkness of hell, the very place that will incarcerate satan, the devil for a thousand years."

Dr. Roger Mills stated that "The Lord God-Jesus spoke and commanded light to come forth, and the whole pit was engulfed in light. Roger could see for the first time while being in the pit. It was a massive prison cell. There were hundreds of jail cells within the sides of the Bottomless Pit. While in the pit, the Lord God-Jesus began to teach Roger about the Bottomless Pit and Armageddon. It was the greatest teaching he have ever heard on those subject matters."

Dr. Roger Mills stated that "The Lord God-Jesus said to me, look, listen, and learn." This is where satan will be imprisoned during the time that I will reign on Earth for a thousand years, in the new Jerusalem, the city of David. This will be after I have raptured the church.

I will tell you what I have not personally told many of my preachers who live in your day and time. The devil, satan does not live in Hell. He has a throne which occupies the second Heaven. He will soon be cast out of the Heavens permanently. Michael and my holy angels will fight against satan and his angels, casting them out of the Heavens, to the Earth. [13]

> Revelation 12:7-9; " [7] *And there was war in heaven: Michael and his angels fought against the dragon; and the dragon fought and his angels,* [8] *And prevailed not; neither was their place found any more in heaven.* [9] *And the great dragon was cast out, that old serpent, called the Devil, and Satan, which deceiveth the whole world: he was cast out into the earth, and his angels were cast out with him."*

Gehenna - The Lake of Fire!

Dr. Roger Mills says he saw the lake of Fire, "it Stretches are far as the eye can see. Looks like volcano erupting.

"…and the Lord God-Jesus asked him, "Would you like to see the lake that burns with fire that is also called the Lake of Fire?"

"The Lord God-Jesus and Roger stated that walked to the entrance of the door and they both looked in, and what he saw reminded him of an ocean that had been set on fire by gasoline. The liquid fire went on as far as the eye could see. It was continuous on length and width. It also reminded him of looking into a volcano erupting." [13]

It is where haters, idol worshipers, adulterers, liars, murderers, thieves, willfully break God's commandments, occult practices are all sent here for second death is the do not repent.

"This place, which is the named 'Gehenna' will one day consume all those who hate their brothers or sisters, who speak from the heart and call their brothers of sisters fools, he or she that blasphemes [speaks against] the name of the Holy Spirit, all those who unrepentantly worship idols, unrepentant liars, unrepentant adulterers, unrepentant thieves, and those who willfully break my commandments."

Roger says… "The Lord God-Jesus explained to him that people who won't repent of the following occult practices will also be cast into this place. [13]

> Matthew 5:22 *"But I say unto you, That whosoever is angry with his brother without a cause shall be in danger of the judgment: and whosoever shall say to his brother, Raca, shall be in danger of the council: but whosoever shall say, Thou fool, shall be in danger of (Gehenna) hell fire."*
>
> Matthew 25:41; *"Then shall he say also unto them on the left hand, Depart from me, ye cursed, into everlasting fire, prepared for the devil and his angels:"*
>
> Revelation 20:10; *"And the devil that deceived them was cast into the lake of fire and brimstone, where the beast and the false prophet are, and shall be tormented day and night forever and ever."*

Chapter 25
The Structure of Hell

Revelation 16:10-11 *And the fifth angel poured out his vial upon the seat of the beast; and his kingdom was full of darkness; and they gnawed their tongues for pain, And blasphemed the God of heaven because of their pains and their sores, and repented not of their deeds.*

Hell is like a human body!

Mary K. Baxter says... "Jesus spoke again, Hell has a body (like a human form) lying on her back in the center of the earth. Hell is shaped like a human body – very large and with many chambers of torment...." [11]

Jesus said, "We are now about to enter a tunnel which will take us into the belly of hell. Hell is shaped like a human body lying in the center of the earth. The body is lying on her back, with both arms and both legs stretched out. As the body of believers, so hell has a body of sin and death. As the Christ-body is built up daily, so the hell-body is also built up daily." [11]

Right Arm of Hell - Not pits, a river, people chained to each other, submerging unbelievers; lovers of flesh; homosexuality.

They walked up a high, dry hill. At the top of the hill, they looked below and saw a swirling river. There were no pits of fire or demons or evil spirits, only the large river flowing between unseen banks. The banks of the river were hidden in the darkness. Jesus and Mary K. Baxter walked closer to the river, and they saw that it was full of blood and fire. As she looked closer, she saw many souls, each chained to another.

The weight of the chains dragged them under the surface of the lake of fire. The souls in hell were in the fire of hell. She saw also that they were in the form of skeletons with misty gray souls. "What is this?" She asked the Lord. "These are the souls of the unbelievers and the ungodly. 11

These individuals were lovers of their own flesh more than lovers of God. They were men loving men, and women loving women, who would not repent and be saved from their sin. They enjoyed their life of sin and spumed God's salvation. "She stood beside Jesus and looked into the lake of fire. The fire began to roar like a great furnace, moving and devouring everything in its path. Soon it filled nearly the entire right arm of hell. The fire approached to within feet of them, but it did not touch them. The river was burning everything in its path. She watched Jesus' face, and it was sad and tender.

He still had love and compassion for these lost souls written on His countenance. Mary began to cry and wished she could leave that place of torment, to go on was almost unbearable. She looked again at the souls in the fire. They were a fiery red, and their bones were blackened and burned. She heard their souls cry out in regret and sorrow. The Lord said, "This is their torment. Chain after chain, they are linked together. These desired the flesh of their own kind, men with men, and women with women, doing that which is unnatural. They led many young girls and young boys into acts of sin. They called it love, but in the end it was sin and death.

She know that many boys and girls, men and women were forced against their wills to commit such atrocious acts She know and will not hold this sin to their charge. Remember this though," said Jesus, "I know all things, and the persons who made these youths to sin have the greater punishment.

Jesus said he will judge righteously. 'to the sinner, He say, 'Repent, and He will have mercy. Call on Him and He will hear. '"Time after time I called to these souls to repent and to come unto Me. I would have forgiven them and cleansed them; and in My name they could have been set free. But they would not listen to Me. They wanted the lust of the flesh more than the love of the living God. Because I am holy, you must be holy. 'touch not the unclean thing, and I will receive you," said the Lord. [11]

Center of Hell

"Witches and sorcerers, murderer who refused to believe when given opportunity, soon we came to the next cell. A desperate cry of sorrow came from within. They looked and saw a skeleton of a man huddled on a floor. His bones were black from burning, and his soul was a dirty gray mist inside. Mary noticed that parts of his body were missing. Smoke and flames came up around him. Worms crawled inside of him. [11]

Jesus said, "This man's sins were many. He was a murderer and hate is in his heart. He would not repent or even believe that I would forgive him. If he had only come to Me!" "You mean, Lord," she asked, "he thought that You would not forgive him of murder and hatred?"

Yes," said Jesus. "If only he had believed and come to Me, He would have forgiven him all his sins, great and small.

Instead, he continued to sin and died in them. That is why he is where he is today. He was given many opportunities to serve Me and to believe the gospel, but he refused. Now it is too late." "A woman's voice said, "Help me." Mary stared into a real pair of eyes, not the burned-out sockets which were the marks of burning. she was so sad she shivered, and Mary felt such pity and sorrow for this soul. Mary wanted so badly to pull her out of the cell and run away with her. "It's so painful," she said. "Lord, she will do what is right now. She once knew the Lord, and He was her Savior." Her hands clenched the bars of the cell. "Why won't you be my Savior now?" Big pieces of burning flesh fell from her, and only bones clenched the bars." [11]

"Jesus even healed her of cancer," she said. "He told me to go and sin no more lest a worse thing come upon me. The lady said she tried, Lord; she said you know I tried. She even tried to witness for Jesus. But, Lord, she soon learned that those who preach His Word are not popular. She wanted people to like her. She slowly went back into the world and the lust of the flesh devoured her. Nightclubs and strong drink became more important than Jesus. She lost touch with her Christian friends and soon found herself seven times worse than she had been before. And though she became lovers of both men and women, she never intended to be lost. She did not know that she was possessed by satan.

She still felt the call of God upon her heart to repent and be saved, but she would not. She kept thinking she still had time. Tomorrow she thought she will turn back to Jesus, and He will forgive her and deliver her. But she waited too long, and now it is too late," she cried. Her sad eyes burst into flames and disappeared. she screamed and fell." [11]

Heart of Hell!

Coming out from this black heart were what shapes that looked like large arms or horns. The arteries are the horns that Daniel saw. Will be used when antichrist rules Earth ahead Mary K. saw a large black object, almost as big as a baseball field which seemed to be moving up and down. She remembered that she had been told this was "the heart of hell."

They were coming out of it and going up and out of hell into the earth and over the earth. She wondered if these horns were the ones the Bible spoke about. All around the heart, the earth was dry and brown. For about thirty feet in all directions, the earth had been burned and had dried to a rusty, brown color. The heart was the blackest of blacks, but another color like the scales of a snake's skin was intermixed with the black. An awful odor arose from the heart each time it beat. It moved as a real heart and beat up and down. An evil force field surrounded it. In amazement Mary K. looked at this evil heart and wondered what its purpose was. Jesus said, "These branches, which look like arteries of a heart, are pipelines that go up through the earth to spill out evil upon it.

These are the horns that Daniel saw, and they represent evil kingdoms on the earth. Some have already been, some shall be, and some are now. Evil kingdoms will arise, and the Antichrist will rule over many peoples, places and things. If possible, the very elect will be deceived by him many will turn away and will worship the beast and his image.

"Out of these main branches or horns, smaller branches will grow. Out of the smaller branches will come demons, evil spirits and all manner of evil forces. They will be released upon the earth and instructed by satan to do many evil works. These kingdoms and evil forces will obey the beast, and many will follow him to destruction. It is here in the heart of hell that these things begin."

Jaws of hell

"As Jesus and Mary K. Baxter continue to walked, they stopped on a hill overlooking a small valley. As far as the eye could see there were piles of human souls lining the sides of this hill. Mark K. Baxter could hear their cries. Loud noises filled the place. Jesus said, "My child, this is the jaws of hell. Every time the mouth of hell is opened, you will hear that loud noise. "The souls were trying to get out but could not, for they were embedded in the sides of hell. As Jesus spoke, Mary K. Baxter saw many dark forms falling down past them and landing with a thud at the bottom of the hill. Demons with great chains were dragging souls away. Jesus said, "Those are the souls that have just died on earth and are arriving in hell. This activity goes on day and night." [11]

Chapter 26
What is it like being in Hell?

1. *A preacher with prejudice and compromise*

"She saw the man's soul inside this skeletal form. He said to the Lord, "Lord, now I will preach the truth to all the people. Now, Lord, I'm ready to go and tell others about this place. I know that while I was on earth, he didn't believe there was a hell, nor did I believe You were coming again. It was what people wanted to hear, and I compromised the truth to the people in my church. I know I didn't like anyone who was different in race or color of skin and I caused many to fall away from You. I made my own rules about heaven and right and wrong. I know that I led many astray, and I caused many to stumble over Your Holy Word, and I took money from the poor. But, Lord, let me out, and I will do right. I won't take money from the church anymore. I have repented already. I will love people of every race and color."[11]

Jesus said, "You not only distorted and misrepresented the Holy Word of God, but you lied about knowing the truth. The pleasures of life were more important to you than truth. I visited you Myself and tried to turn you around, but you would not listen. You went your own way, and evil was your lord. You knew the truth, but you would not repent or turn back to me. I was there all the time. I waited for you. I wanted you to repent, but you did not. And now the judgment has been set."
[11]

2. Woman, you are still full of lies and sin.

We stopped at the next pit. It was exactly like all the others. Inside it was the form of a woman, which I knew by her voice. She cried out to Jesus for deliverance from the flames. Jesus looked on the woman with love and said, "While you were on earth, I called you to come to Me. I pleaded with you to get your heart right with Me before it was too late. I visited you many times in the midnight hour to tell you of My love. I wooed you, loved you and drew you to Me by My Spirit. "Yes Lord,' you said, 'I will follow You,' With your lips you said you loved Me, but your heart did not mean it. I knew where your heart was. I often sent my messengers to you to tell you to repent of your sins and come to Me, but you would not hear Me. I wanted to use you to minister to others, to help others to find Me. But you wanted the world and not Me. I called you, but you would not hear Me, nor would you repent of your sins. "The woman said to Jesus, "You remember, Lord, how I went to church and was a good woman. I joined the church. I was a member of Your church. I knew Your call was on my life. I knew I had to obey that call at all costs, and I did. "Jesus said, "Woman, you are still full of lies and sin." [11] I called you, but you would not hear Me! True, you were a member of a church, but being a church member did not get you to heaven. Your sins were many, and you did not repent. You caused others to stumble at My Word.

You would not forgive others when they hurt you. You pretended to love and serve Me when you were with Christians, but when you were away from Christians, you lied, cheated and stole. You gave heed to seducing spirits and enjoyed your double life. You knew the straight and narrow way."

Jesus said, "you also had a double tongue. You talked about your brothers and sisters in Christ. You judged them and thought you were holier than they, when there was gross sin in your heart. This I know, you would not listen to My sweet Spirit of compassion. You judged the outside of a person, without regard to the fact that many were children in the faith. You were very hard. "Yes, you said you loved Me with your lips, but your heart was far from Me. You knew the ways of the Lord and you understood. You played with God, and God knows all things. If you had sincerely served God, you would not be here today. You cannot serve Satan and God at the same time.

"Jesus turned to me and said, "Many in the last days will depart from the faith, giving heed to seducing spirits and will serve sin. Come out from among them, and be separate. Walk not in the way with them." As we walked away, the woman began to curse and swear at Jesus. She screamed and cried with rage. Take heed you ministers of the gospel, for these are faithful and true sayings. Awake, evangelists, preachers, and teachers of My Word, all of you who are called to preach the gospel of the Lord Jesus Christ! If you are sinning, repent or you will likewise perish." [11]

3. This man was a preacher of the Word of God.

We walked up to within fifteen feet of this activity. I saw small dark-clothed figures marching around a boxlike object. Upon closer examination, I saw that the box was a coffin and the figures marching around it were demons. It was a real coffin, and there were twelve demons marching around it. As they marched, they were chanting and laughing. Each one had a sharp spear in his hand, which he kept thrusting into the coffin through small openings that lined the outside. There was a feeling of great fear in the air, and I trembled at the sight before me. Jesus knew my thoughts, for He said, "Child, there are many souls in torment here, and there are many different types of torment for these souls. There is greater punishment for those who once preached the gospel and went back into sin, or for those who would not obey the call of God for their lives.

"I heard a cry so desperate that it filled my heart with despair. "No hope, no hope!" he called. The hopeless cry came from the coffin. It was an endless wail of regret. "Oh, how awful!" I said. "Come," said Jesus, "let's go closer." With that, He walked up to the coffin and looked inside. I followed and also looked in. It appeared that the evil spirits could not see us.

A dirty-gray mist filled the inside of the coffin. It was the soul of a man. As I watched, the demons pushed their spears into the soul of the man in the coffin. I will never forget the suffering of this soul. I cried to Jesus, "Let him out, Lord; let him out. "The torment of his soul was such a terrible sight. If only he could get free. I pulled at Jesus' hand and begged Him to let the man out of the coffin. Jesus said, "My child, peace, be still."

As Jesus spoke, the man saw us. He said, "Lord, Lord, let me out. Have mercy." I looked down and saw a bloody mess. Before my eyes was a soul. Inside the soul was a human heart, and blood spurted from it. The thrusting of the spears was literally piercing his heart.

"I will serve You now, Lord." He begged, "Please let me out." I knew that this man felt every spear that pierced his heart. "Day and night, he is tormented," the Lord said. "He was put here by Satan, and it is Satan who torments him." The man cried, "Lord, I will now preach the true gospel. I will tell about sin and hell. But please help me out of here."

Jesus said, "This man was a preacher of the Word of God. There was a time when he served Me with all his heart and led many people to salvation. Some of his converts are still serving Me today, many years later. The lust of the flesh and the deceitfulness of riches led him astray. He let Satan gain the rule over him. He had a big church, a fine car, a large income. He began to steal from the church offerings. He began to teach lies. He spoke mostly half-lies and half-truths. He would not let Me correct him. I sent My messengers to him to tell him to repent and preach the truth, but he loved the pleasures of this life more than the life of God.

He knew not to teach or preach any other doctrine except the truth as revealed in the Bible. But before he died, he said the Holy Ghost baptism was a lie and that those who claimed to have the Holy Ghost were hypocrites. He said you could be a drunkard and get to heaven, even without repentance." He said God would not send anyone to hell - that God was too good to do that. He caused many good people to fall from the grace of the Lord. He even said that he did not need Me, for he was like a god. He went so far as to hold seminars to teach this false doctrine. He trampled My Holy Word under his feet. Yet, I continued to love him. "My child, it is better to have never known Me than to know Me and turn back from serving Me," said the Lord.

"If only he had listened to You, Lord!" I cried. "If only he had cared about his soul and the souls of others." "He did not listen to Me. When I called he would not hear Me. He loved the easy life. I called and called him to repentance, but he would not come back to Me. One day he was killed and came immediately here. Now Satan torments him for having once preached My Word and saved souls for my kingdom. This is his torment." I watched the demons as they continued to march around and around the coffin. The man's heart beat and real blood ran from it. I will never forget his cries of pain and sorrow. Jesus looked at the man in the coffin with great compassion and said, "The blood of many lost souls is upon this man's hands. Many of them are in torment here right now." With sorrowful hearts, Jesus and I walked on. As we left, I saw another group of demons coming up to the coffin. They were about three feet high, dressed in black clothes, with black hoods over their faces, they were taking shifts tormenting him.

4. Witch from family of witches, refused Jesus, witch, who taught, brought 500 souls to Satan; fully deceived; sold soul.

"As we walked along the ledge, the sounds grew louder. Great cries came from inside the cells. As I walked close to Jesus, He stopped in front of the third cell. A bright light illumined the inside of the cell. In the cell was an old woman sitting in a rocking chair, rocking and crying as though her heart would break. I don't know why, but I was shocked to find that this woman was a real person with a body. The cell was completely bare except for the woman in the rocking chair. The walls of the cell were constructed of light clay and dirt, molded into the earth. The front door spanned the entire front of the cell. It was made of black metal with bars of metal and a lock on it. Since the bars were set wide apart, Jesus and I had an almost unlimited view of the entire cell." The old woman's color was ashen-flesh mixed with a grayish tint. She was rocking back and forth. As she rocked, tears rolled down her cheeks. I knew from her agonized expression that she was in great pain and was suffering from some unseen torment. I wondered what she had been charged with that she should be imprisoned here.

All of a sudden, right before my eyes, the woman began to change forms - first to an old man, and then to a young woman to a middle-aged woman and then back to the old lady I had first seen. In shock, I watched as she went through these changes one after the other. When she saw Jesus, she cried, "Lord, have mercy on me. Let me out of this place of torment." She leaned forward in her chair and reached for Jesus, but could not get to Him.

The changing continued. Even her clothes changed, so that she was attired as a man, then a young girl, a middle aged woman and an old woman in turn. All of this changing seemed to take only a few minutes.

I asked Jesus, "Why, Lord?" Again she screamed, "O Lord, let me out of here before they return." She now stood at the front of the cell, clenching the bars with tight fists. She said, "I know Your love is real. I know Your love is true. Let me out!" Then as the woman cried in terror, I saw that something was beginning to rip the flesh from her body.

"She is not what she appears to be," said the Lord.

The woman sat back in the chair and began to rock. But now only a skeleton was sitting in the rocking chair-a skeleton with a dirty mist inside. Where there had been a clothed body only minutes ago, now there were blackened and burned bones and empty sockets for eyes. The soul of the woman moaned and cried out to Jesus in repentance. But her cries were too late.

5. German witch who committed suicide to be able to raise self from dead.

"This woman was a witch while back on Earth. She lived in Germany. She knew about my Holy Word. Her grandmother taught her all about my Holy Word, of which you call the Bible. She became involved in Astrology and became heavily involved in spells. She had learned how to cast spells on people. She no longer has interest in my Holy Word, not in the church. In fact, she would even go so far as to try to use my Holy Word to cast spells on certain persons. I send many witnesses to her, to tell her to stop, but she would not listen. Her witchcraft grew worse and worse. She began to talk to demon spirits and they told her that if she would kill herself, she would have the power to raise herself from the dead, and have even greater power as a witch. ... Convinced, she used a knife from within her kitchen, cutting her wrists and committing suicide."[13]

6. Mission to feed the poor, the man stole money to finance big home.

The Lord God-Jesus said, "What you have just seen was a man who I called to serve me by means of helping to feed the poor. He started a small mission and gained my favor. I caused many people to contribute money to his mission. For years, he raised a lot of money in the name of the poor and opened up a soup kitchen, but he took more than half the money for himself. He knew that stealing money from the poor was wrong because I came to him on numerous occasions and convicted him by my Spirit…His conscience bothered him for a while, but still he did not repent. He bought an expensive home and cars with the mission's money. [13]

7. Backsliding woman cut apart with chainsaw.

"She had been saved but wanted a man who was a sorcerer "Maria, I called you to teach the gospel, as I did many other members of your family. Unlike you, they listened to me and obeyed the calling I placed upon their lives. …you knew right from wrong. You heard the gospel preached on numerous occasions. Then Satan deceived you one day. He used a tall, handsome man to entice you away from your local church. Satan seduced your heart to fall in love with that young man….eventually you married him, and got involved with practicing black magic.

I watched as you mother, our sisters and many of your friends warned you about the young man and his involvement with the occult. He was involved in all sorts of magic, black magic in particular. He became a wizard and a sorcerer….You blamed me for the physical, verbal and mental abuse he inflicted on you….one day he came home in a drunken rage and he murdered you by sawing you in half with a chainsaw. … as I told you before, when you first arrived here, I did not send you to this place of torment in Hell. You sent yourself."[13]

8. Preacher who preached once save always saved and what people wanted to hear for more income.

"The Lord God-Jesus said to me, "This man was a servant of mine while he was on Earth. He was an ordained preacher who was Pastoring a church that had 25 members. "…He was one of my servants who was unhappy with Pastoring a small church. He complained about the church's income, that it was not enough.

So I showed him in my Holy Word where I had said well done, good and faithful servant; though hast been faithful over a few things, I will make thee ruler over many things; enter thou into the joy of thy Lord." *Matthew 25:23*

"However he was not patient, so he began to stop preaching the truth and he told lies to the people. … He said within his heart, 'If I preach to people only about things they want to here, then I will have a large church.'

His church did in fact increase with members. …His heart was also filled with lies, and he no longer spoke the truth about me as the only savior of humanity. He preached to his congregation that there are many ways to God …He also preached the message to many that once saves, you are always saved, and that no matter what you cannot lose your salvation.…He became rich from that type of preaching. I came to him many times by my Holy Spirit to tell him to stop doing wrong, but he would not listen."[13]

9. A Christian Women healed of Cancer

Mary Baxter shared of women that she saw in hell. A woman's voice said, "Help me." I stared into a real pair of eyes, not the burned-out sockets which were the marks of burning. I was so sad I shivered, and I felt such pity and sorrow for this soul. I wanted so badly to pull her out of the cell and run away with her. "It's so painful," she said.

"Lord, I will do what is right now. I once knew You, and You were my Savior." Her hands clenched the bars of the cell. "Why won't you be my Savior now?" Big pieces of burning flesh fell from her, and only bones clenched the bars.

" You even healed me of cancer," she said. "You told me to go and sin no more lest a worse thing come upon me. I tried, Lord; You know I tried. I even tried to witness for You. But, Lord, I soon learned that those who preach Your Word are not popular. I wanted people to like me. I slowly went back into the world and the lust of the flesh devoured me. Nightclubs and strong drink became more important than You. I lost touch with my Christian friends and soon found myself seven times worse than I had been before.

"And though I became lovers of both men and women, I never intended to be lost. I did not know that I was possessed by satan. I still felt Your call upon my heart to repent and be saved, but I would not. I kept thinking I still had time. Tomorrow I will turn back to Jesus, and He will forgive me and deliver me. But I waited too long, and now it is too late," she cried.

Her sad eyes burst into flames and disappeared. I screamed and fell against Jesus. [11]

A short summary of the testimony by Victoria Nehale

Victoria was born and lived in Namibia all my life and surrendered my life to Jesus on February 06, 2005. The Lord Jesus Christ has revealed many things in the spiritual realm to me including a couple of trips to hell. The Lord instructed me to share my experiences with the people; He also warned me not to add anything or omit anything from whatever the Lord Jesus Christ showed or told me. She was visited 33 times by the Lord Jesus Christ. Every single time of those visitations, the Lord would tell me before leaving that:

On the weekend of 23 July 2005, she took a thirty-minute taxi ride from the town of Ondangwa where she work and stay, to my home village, to spend the weekend with my parents. On my way home, she had a feeling that something extraordinary was going to happen that evening. She arrived home at around 6:00 pm and that was the time people were preparing for dinner. She was in the kitchen with the rest of my family, lying down on an old sheet on the ground, while my little nieces and nephews were singing their Sunday School songs. Suddenly She felt a heavy anointing come upon me, my body became very weak, and she was out under the power of God. She saw a man, wearing a long white robe tied with a rope of the same color, walking towards where she was lying. There was a brilliant light around Him as though it were radiating from Him. He was wearing brown sandals; His features were like people from the Middle East, with a beautiful tanned skin. His face was very kind and full of glory but she was unable to look Him in the eyes.

When He spoke, His voice was tender, kind and loving, yet authoritative; waves of love were emanating from His very being. He extended His hand to me and pulled me up from where I was lying. Suddenly I was in a beautiful, transformed body; I looked the same as I was when I was eighteen years old. I was wearing a white robe tied with a white rope. Although my robe was white, the material was different from the man's robe. His robe was silky with a brilliance that I do not know how to describe.

He said, in a most loving and tender voice: *"Victoria, I want you to come with me; I will show you frightening things and I am taking you to a place where you have never been before in your whole life"*.

He held my right hand and we went. I felt as if we were walking on air and we were ascending all the time. After a while on the way, I was very tired and told Him that I was unable to continue the journey and begged Him to allow me to go back. However, He looked at me tenderly and said, *"You are not tired - you are fine. If you get tired, I will carry you, but for now you are fine. Peace be with you. Let us go."*

The place at which we arrived was very arid, worse than the worst desert known to man, with no sign of life in any form whatsoever. There was not a single tree or blade of grass or any living thing in sight. It was a very depressing place indeed.

We came to a gate and the man turned to me and said: *"Victoria, we will enter through the gate and the things you will see will frighten and upset you - but you must rest assured that wherever I take you, you will be well protected. Just open your eyes and observe everything I will show you."*

Victoria was terrified and started to weep. I was protesting and pleaded with the man to take me back. She told Him that she did not want to go into that place because she could see through the gate what was going on inside.

He looked at me and said, *"Peace be with you; I am with you. We must go inside, for time is fast running out."*

We entered through the gate. She cannot describe to you the horror of that place. I am convinced that there is no other place in the entire universe as bad as that place. The place was extremely large and I had the sense that it was expanding all the time. It was a place of utmost darkness and the heat of it could not be measured: it was hotter than the hottest of fires. I could not see any flames of fire or the source of the heat but it was HOT. The place was filled with flies of all sizes - green, black, and grey flies. Every conceivable kind of fly was there.

In addition, there were also short, thick, black worms everywhere, climbing on everything. The worms started to climb on us and the flies were also all over us. The place was filled with the most disgusting stench; there are no words to describe the intensity of the stench in that place. The smell was almost like rotten meat but was a hundred times worse than the most decaying meat I have ever smelled in my entire life. The place was filled with the noise of wailing and gnashing of teeth, as well as of demonic, evil laughter.

The worst thing about this place is that it was filled with people. There were so many people that they could not be numbered. The people were in the form of skeletons.

Victoria can say with confidence that these skeletons were humans because I recognized some of my very close relatives and people from my village. Their bones were dark grey and extremely dry. They had long sharp teeth like wild animals.

Their mouths were large and wide and their tongues were long and bright red. Their hands and feet had long, thin toes and fingers with long, sharp nails. Some of them had tails and horns.

There were demons mingling with the people: the demons in appearance looked like alligators and they were walking on four legs. They were comfortable in that environment and were constantly teasing and tormenting the humans.

The noise that the demons were making was more like a celebration, as they seemed happy and carefree; they were also dancing and jumping all the time. The humans, on the other hand, looked miserable and depressed; they were in a state of helplessness and hopelessness. The noise from humans was caused by pain; they were weeping, screaming and gnashing their teeth, and were in a desperate situation of unimaginable pain and agony.

The people in this place, were innumerable but I could clearly see that the vast majority of them were women. They were divided into many different groups. Even if they were in the groups, it was not possible to estimate the number of people in any single group because the groups were extremely large. The man led me to one of the groups on the eastern side of the place.

He looked at me and said: *"Victoria, this is a group of people who refused to forgive others. I told them many times in many different ways to forgive others but they rejected me; I have forgiven them all their sins but they refused to forgive others. Their time ran out and they found themselves here. They will be here for all eternity; they are eating the fruits of their labour forever and ever. However, it is painful for me to see them in this horrible place and in this eternal situation - because I love them."*

I was then led to the next group, and the man told me that the people in the second group were those who had debts. There were three different categories in that group.

The **first category** was of people who owed to others: they could afford to pay their dues but they kept postponing and procrastinating. They would claim that they would pay tomorrow, next week, next year, until the time ran out for them and now they had found themselves in this place. This is where they will stay forever; they are eating the fruits of their labour.

The **second category** was of those who had debts that they could afford to pay back and they were willing to pay their debts, but they were afraid of the consequences because, perhaps, if they told the truth they might suffer rejection or they might go to jail or what they had done would be made known to the whole world and they would be humiliated.

The man said: *"None of them came to me to ask me for a way. If they had done so, I would have shown them the easy way out. They used their own wisdom and reasoning which did not help them in any way. Their time ran out and they found themselves in this place where they will be forever. They are eating the fruit of their labour."*

Then He said: *"The* **third category** *had debts which they could not afford to pay back, but, again, none of them had told me that they had debts they were unable to pay. If they had done so, I would have paid their debts. They also tried to use their own reasoning and wisdom, which did not help them in any way. Now they have found themselves in this place where they will always be. They are eating the fruit of their labour. My heart is aching for all these people because I love them dearly."*

In the **first group**, I saw two of my very close female relatives, as well as a *twelve year-old*, also a relative of mine. I knew she was twelve because that was how old she was at the time of her death. In the second group I also saw some of my relatives, as well as a Pastor whom I knew very well, Jakes, my boyfriend who had committed suicide because I gave my life to Christ.

The **second group**, I saw some of my neighbors in both groups as well. I recognized the people I knew before their deaths; they also recognized me. My relatives were very angry when they saw me and they started to shout obscenities at me; they were using the most vulgar language as they were cursing me. One of them said that I was not worthy of following the man who was with me; they were telling the things I used to do before I gave my life to Christ.

They were not lying; the things of which they were accusing me were the truth. Jakes was saying that I belonged to him and I should go where he was because I had committed the same sins as he.

At first the Pastor seemed happy to see me and he said I did well by coming but his attitude changed immediately when he saw who was accompanying me and then he also joined in the cursing and the use of obscene language. The man with me told me to ignore them for they did not know what they were doing. I was petrified and extremely sad; my body was shaking and I could not stand. I was crying uncontrollably.

The man turned to me, gave me a hug, and said: *"Peace be with you, Victoria."* My strength returned and I felt very secure in His embrace. Then He told me that we had to leave the place and go back. He looked at me and said: *"Victoria, I have shown you. Now you must choose in which of the groups you want to be; the choice is in your own hands. You must tell the people everything you have seen and experienced but do not add or omit anything."*

I remembered that we left the place of horrors together but I do not know where I left Him because then I became aware: I opened my eyes and I was back in my physical body, lying in Oshakati Hospital. There was a drip in my left arm, and I saw my mother and other neighbors from our village in one corner of the room, where they were looking at me in amazement. I could see on my mother's face that she had been crying. They asked one of the nurses if she knew what was wrong with me but she only made a joke and said: "You were sent back; perhaps you have done something wrong and you need to repent."

The nurse was trying to speak lightheartedly about my condition but I could see she was afraid to come closer to me. I asked her to call the doctor who attended me.

When he arrived, he said that he did not know what was wrong with me. Initially, he had thought that I had contracted malaria but the malaria results were negative. He continued to tell me that my temperature, pulse and blood pressure were dangerously low but he could not find the cause for it. He said that there was nothing he could do for me; he could not admit me because I was not sick. The drip they had applied was not working at first but when I opened my eyes, it started to work. He recommended that the nurse administered another drip to me once the first one had finished so that I could get enough strength to go home. I was frightened by what I saw in that place and couldn't stop crying.

The stench of that horrible place continued to be as real as when I was there. The scenes from that place were flashing before me all the time. I was unable to sleep and my whole body was in great pain. I felt as though all my limbs had been taken apart, and reassembled. Oh, I felt awful. I had diarrhea and a pounding headache for an entire week.

My mind was made up that I would not talk to anybody about my experiences because who would believe me? What would people think? I kept telling myself that I would never relate my experiences to anybody. One of my mentors phoned me three days later to enquire about my wellbeing because I sent her a text message asking her to pray for me. Before I knew it I was telling her about my experiences.

When I realized what I was doing I had already told her most of the story. I wanted to kick myself. I was crying because I was convinced that I had made the biggest mistake of my life.

Now the story was told, there was no possibility I could hide it anymore. Now I knew that if God wants something to be told, it will be told. He is God, after all.

On August 19, I woke up, feeling the signs of the anointing in my physical body. I was weak and trembling, while waves of electricity were going through my body. In the evening I saw a brilliant light coming into the room and in the midst of it was the same man. This time He sat down on a chair next to my bed. I have no idea where this chair came from but it was there as soon as He was ready to sit down. It was a beautiful chair made of solid gold; the shape was that of a conventional chair, with back support.

On each leg was a silver star embedded in the gold; the same star was also in the centre of the back support. There are round wheels on each leg. After greeting me, He told me that He knew that I had many questions about His identity and that He came to reveal Himself to me and to explain certain things that I have experienced.

He said: *"I am Jesus Christ, your Saviour. If you have any doubts, look at my hands. That place where we went is Hell."* When I looked at His hands, I saw scars where the nails pierced Him.

Dear friend, I want to tell you that hell is not a figment of anybody's imagination but it is a real place and it is unpleasant. It was not made for people but for Satan and his demons. Our rightful place is in Heaven with Jesus but we have to choose Jesus before it is too late. Today, when you hear His voice, do not harden your heart; accept Jesus as your personal Saviour today and live for Him.

Hell is a terrible place: it is a place of fear and sadness; it is a place of torment and eternal cries and gnashing of teeth. Satan wants to take as many people with him as possible. Do not co-operate with him; co-operate with Jesus and you will live and not die. I could not understand why the Lord would tell me to make a choice between the two groups He showed me in Hell when I was already a born-again Christian. I have accepted Him into my life and He was still telling me to make a choice whether I want to go to Hell or not. I could not understand. I started to pray and asked God to give me a revelation of what He meant and what He wanted me to do.

The Lord revealed to me that I was harboring a lack of forgiveness and resentment in my heart towards one of my sisters, as well as to my cousin. I asked the Lord to forgive me for my unforgiving spirit; I also asked my sister to forgive me for harboring anger and bitterness in my heart toward her. The Lord instructed me to go and ask forgiveness from my cousin.

The Lord also reminded me that there was a time when I acquired a teaching job with a fraudulent diploma and He considered that to be debt and theft. I was determined to do what was right and I asked the Lord to help me through this problem and to show me an easy way out because this was a serious crime which could send me behind bars. He directed me to go to the Department of Education and confess what I had done. I was ready to go to jail if this was unavoidable. I experienced the Lord's favour in a big way.

The officials in the Department of Education told me that I should decide what I wanted to do: whether to pay back the salary I had received from the government or not. They promised not press charges against me because they were stunned by my confession. Our God is a faithful God who honors His Word.

If you are in a situation similar to the one I was in, I want to encourage you to do what is right, no matter the consequences. You might be incarcerated in the earthly jail but that is temporal. No pain or shame will compare to Eternity separated from God. Hell is not a nice place: it is better to allow God to judge you now before it is too late. We must not fear God's judgment while we are in the time of Grace: we must allow Him to expose whatever is wrong in our lives while we still have time to make right with Him because there is no forgiveness on the other side of the grave.

Chapter 27
How to get to Heaven and escape hell?

As we have shared with you about Heaven Blessings beyond the Blue, and The Horror beneath the Grave. Heaven is a real place where God is with all his attributes. Hell is a place with the opposite attributes. According to the scriptures we have a clear understanding of those attributes. Here are some of the attributes listed below:

God is love, hell is a place of hatred, God is light, hell is a place of darkness, God is life and peace, hell is a place of death and confusion, God is merciful, hell is a place with no mercy, God is strong, hell is a place of weakness, God blessed heaven with a awesome atmosphere with a great fragrance, hell is a place of awful odor with horror stench, God is a giver of water, hell is a place of no water, God is a giver of sweet sleep, hell is a place of no rest, God provides food for the hungry, hell is a place of no food, God provides mansion, in hell you are place in a barred pit, God provides a place of pleasure, hell is a place of torment, God provides a place of fellowship, and hell is a place isolation.

HEAVEN IS A *PREPARED* PLACE FOR A *PREPARED* PEOPLE WHO WANT TO SPEND ETERNITY WITH GOD AND ENJOY HIS *PRESENCE* AND PROVISIONS.

Hell was prepared for the devil and his angels according Matthew 25:41; Also anyone who does not want to be with God, the GREAT JEHOVAH, and the way that you show that you don't want to be with God is by not receiving His Son, the Lord Jesus Christ as their Savior. Hell is a prepared place for those who don't want to be in God presence, and enjoy His provisions.

The CHOICE IS YOURS, the only person that sent to hell was His Son JESUS to take our place so that we don't have to go! Our part is to receive His Son as our own personal Lord and Saviour. Whereby we can spend eternity with God, the GREAT JEHOVAH based upon our relationship with Him through His Son JESUS who is the Christ.

God has provided us with an opportunity to have a personal relationship with Him through His Son the Lord Jesus Christ.

From any address in the world, *Jesus said unto him (Thomas)...* "I am the way, the truth, and the life: no man cometh unto the Father, but by me." *John 14:6;*

> In **Acts 4:12**, the scripture says… "Neither is there salvation in any other: for there is none other name under heaven given among men, whereby we must be saved."

Heavenly Decision

To receive Jesus Christ as your own personal Lord and Savior

Are you born again? Have you ever received Jesus as your Lord and Savior? If the answer to this question is no, read these scriptures and pray this prayer, agreeing with it and believing it from your heart

John 3:16 "For God so loved the world, that he gave his only begotten Son, that whosoever believeth in him should not perish, but have everlasting life"

Romans 10:9-10, 13 "That if thou shalt confess with thy mouth the Lord Jesus, and shalt believe in thine heart that God hath raised him from the dead, thou shalt be saved. For whosoever shall call upon the name of the Lord shall be saved. For with the heart man believeth unto righteousness; and with the mouth **Confession** is made unto salvation.

Pray this pray now: Salvation

Dear God,

I want to become a citizen of your Kingdom. I come to you in the name of Jesus, your son. I confess I am a sinner. I believe you sent your son to die on the cross for my sins. I confess with my mouth that Jesus Christ is Lord. Thank you for allowing me to become a Christian; I am translated from the kingdom of darkness to the Kingdom of God.

In Jesus' name I pray, Amen!

As a genuine born-again Christian, a citizen of the Kingdom of God wants, above everything else, to do the will of God. Don't be ashamed to witness to others and tell them how to become a Christian. Join a Bible believing Church and be water baptized as an act of faith to let the world know you are following Christ's example.

Signed _____
Date _____

If you would like to receive the Holy Spirit, ask the Father in Jesus' name to fill you with the Holy Spirit. Believe you receive when you ask, and begin to speak your new language in faith as God gives it to you.

Pray this pray now: Receive the fullness of the Holy Spirit

Heavenly Father,

I come to you in faith, believing that Jesus Christ died in my place, for my sins, and arose from the dead. I ask you to fill me to overflowing with the Holy Spirit. You said in your Word that if I asked I would receive, so I ask you now to fill me to overflowing with your precious Holy Spirit. I receive Him now by faith and expect to speak with other tongues as he gives me the utterance. In Jesus' Name Amen

Pray this pray now: Receive healing

Now I want you to pray for your healing. Put your hand on your body where you are sick and repeat this prayer: Lord Jesus you are the Great Physician. All healing comes from you. By your stripes we are healed. I speak your Word over this body and thank you that you heal all our diseases. Thank you for healing and enabling me to walk in health. In Jesus' Name Amen

Endnotes

1. Bible, King James Vision
2. Gary Wood, *A place called heaven* (Tate Publishing & Enterprises, LLC 2008).
3. Choo Thomas, *Heaven is so real* (Charisma House, 2003, 2006)
4. Mary Baxter, *A Divine Revelation of Heaven* (Whitaker House, 1998).
5. Jesse Duplantis, *Heaven- Close Encounters of the God Kind* (Tulsa, OK: Harrison House, 1996)
6. Roberts Liardon, *We saw Heaven* (Shippensburg, PA: Destiny Image, 2000).
7. Bishop Earthquake Kelley, *Bound to Lose Destined to Win (CopperScroll Publishers, LLC, 2007)*
8. Rebecca Ruter Springer, *Intra Muros* (Colorado Spring, David C. Cook Publishing Company, 1898)
9. Shawn Bolz, (*Keys* to Heaven's Economy an Angelic Visitation from the Minister of Finance, Streams Publishing House, 2005)
10. Marietta Davis, Caught Up Into Heaven (New Kensington, PA: Whitaker House, 1999)
11. Mary Baxter, *A Divine Revelation of Hell* (Whitaker House, 1997).
12. Bill Wiese, *23 Minutes in Hell* (Lake Mary, Florida: Charisma House, 2006)

13. Dr. Roger Mills, *While Out of My Body I Saw God Hell and the Living Dead* (St. Clair Shores, MI: Triunity Publishing Inc., 2007)

14. Howard O. Pittman, *Placebo* (Foxworth, Mississippi: New Philadelphian Publishing House, 1999)

15. Maurice S. Rawlings, M.D, *To Hell and Back* (Nashville, Tennessee: Thomas Nelson Inc., Publisher 1993)

16. Beth Ann Jones, *Hell How could a loving God send anyone there?* (Beth Jones Ministries, Publisher 2007)

17. Dean Braxton "Gets a glimpse of Heaven http://newstalkcleveland.com /2414162/during-routine-surgery-dean-braxton-gets-a-glimpse-of-heaven-and-his-life-is-changed-forever/

18. Freddy Vest "A Rodeo Cowboy's Fight to Survive" http://www.cbn.com/700club/features/amazing/AR99_Freddy_Vest.aspx

19. Victoria Nehale "Time is Running out" http://www.heavenvist.com/Victoria_hale.php

20. Ricarado Cid "8 Hours in Heaven" http://www. Ricarado Cid.com/Ricarado

21. Norvel Hayes, Stand In Gap For Your Children, Harrison House, Tulsa Oklahoma, 1983

About the Author

Pastor James L. Monteria is born again and ordained Minister of the Gospel. He is a graduate of Rhema Bible Training Center of Broken Arrow a suburb of Tulsa, Oklahoma where he earned a Diploma in Ministerial Training. Pastor Monteria received his Bachelor's of Science Degree in Business Administration from Saint Paul's College in Lawrenceville, VA. He received a Master's Degree in Instructional Education from Central Michigan University, Mount Pleasant, Michigan. Pastor Monteria has ministered the Word of God through seminars, church services, Bible studies, Prison Ministries, distributions of his books, CD's and DVD's.

Pastor Monteria believes that the Bible is the Word of God, and he is an anointed Pastor and Teacher of the Word of God. His ministries are combination of anointed Preaching and Teaching the Word of God; and flowing in the gifts of the Holy Spirit as the lead.

PASTOR J. L. MONTERIA IS AVAILABLE FOR

~SPEAKING ENGAGEMENTS~
~BOOK SIGNINGS~
~WORKSHOPS\CONFERENCES~

YOU MAY CONTACT J L MONTERIA VIA

EMAIL: COMEANDLEARNOFME@GMAIL.COM

POSTAL MAIL: P. O. BOX 932 CHESTERFIELD, VA 23832

WEBSITE: WWW.CLMMINISTRIES.ORG

www.ingramcontent.com/pod-product-compliance
Lightning Source LLC
Chambersburg PA
CBHW070813100426
42742CB00012B/2348